THE MOUNTAINS OF SNOWDONIA IN ART

The Visualisation of Mountain Scenery from the
Mid-Eighteenth Century to the Present Day

First published in 2015

© Peter Bishop

© Gwasg Carreg Gwalch 2015

All rights reserved. No part of this publication
may be reproduced, stored in a retrieval system,
or transmitted in any form or by any means, electronic,
electrostatic, magnetic tape, mechanical, photocopying,
recording, or otherwise, without prior permission
of the authors of the works herein.

ISBN: 978-1-84524-227-5

COVER IMAGE
John Warwick Smith, *An Ascent of Snowdon*, 1790, watercolour
© The Trustees of the British Museum

COVER DESIGN
Eleri Owen, Pwllheli

Published by Gwasg Carreg Gwalch,
12 Iard yr Orsaf, Llanrwst, Wales LL26 0EH
tel: 01492 642031
fax: 01492 641502
email: books@carreg-gwalch.com
internet: www.carreg-gwalch.com

The Mountains of Snowdonia in Art

The Visualisation of Mountain Scenery from the Mid-Eighteenth Century to the Present Day

PETER BISHOP

By the same author:

*'Rich and Varied Prospects' Mountain Scenery in Snowdonia 1764-1836:
Thomas Pennant's 'A Tour in Wales' and its Influence.*
MA thesis, University of Central England in Birmingham 1995

Vision and Revision: Mountain Scenery in Snowdonia 1750–1880.
PhD thesis, University of Wales, Aberystwyth 2001

Peter Bishop: Cader Idris
Exhibition catalogue, Peter Bishop 2012, ISBN 978-0-9571788-0-9

Peter Bishop, Cader Idris, Llyn y Cau, *2011,
watercolour and charcoal on paper, 32 x 42, collection of the artist*

Richard Wilson, Llyn y Cau, Cader Idris, *c1765-7,*
oil on canvas, 50 x 72, Tate Britain

'Mountains are the beginning and the end of all natural scenery.'
John Ruskin, Modern Painters, Vol. 4, 'Of Mountain Beauty'. London, 1856.

Contents

Foreword		8
Preface		11
Acknowledgements		12
Introduction		14
One	A View in Nant Peris: A Topographical Viewpoint (Plates 1-6)	18
Two	Snowdon from Capel Curig: A Classical Viewpoint (Plates 7-12)	32
Three	Views of Snowdon (Plates 13-23)	46
Four	Sketching on the Move (Plates 24-30)	70
Five	Views of Cader Idris (Plates 31-39)	86
Six	Pont Aberglaslyn: A Picturesque Viewpoint (Plates 40-47)	106
Seven	Llyn Idwal: A Sublime Viewpoint (Plates 48-57)	124
Eight	Arenig Fawr: A Painter's Mountain (Plates 58-63)	150
Nine	Betws-y-coed and its Mountain Scenery (Plates 64-69)	164
Endnotes		180
Further Reading		180
Index of Artist Entries		181
Glossary of Terms		182
Select Bibliography		185
List of Illustrated Works		188

Foreword

Mountain

Peter Bishop and I were fellow painting students at the Slade in the early seventies. For many years mountains have been the subject of his paintings, and especially the mountains of Snowdonia. It is typical of his single-mindedness and devotion that he should follow his passion as an artist with such depth of research. This book is proof of how he has made this region in art his own.

I am sitting in a small cottage on Anglesey looking out towards Snowdonia. Each morning the brilliant and transfiguring light from the east seems to confirm it as the proper home of the gods. Yet I have also spent days looking hopefully towards Snowdon while the summit is invisible, and a week once without even glimpsing it. In two weeks of continual rain when walking the Cambrian Way, hardly a peak existed until abandoning the trail for the coast and the Llŷn peninsula I looked back to see an entire range clear in the sunshine. In these northern climes the sublimity and portentousness of the idea competes vigorously with the knee-jarring substance of the reality. Close up under the walking boot the mountain is a mere small patch of rock, grit, mud or peat - an experience accompanied by mild resentment or, occasionally, anguish. Amongst the rainy hills of mid Wales it seems only changeability is permanent. Given art's trope of defying time, the mountain as eternal symbol is the perfect painting subject, yet how often it turns the visual artist more into a hunter than an observer. I am reminded how odd the mountain is as a subject for painting. Remote by definition, it is both the greatest object and the greatest subject and for art one of the most unsuitable and elusive.

Unlike the human face or figure, the room, the house, or even such another object of vastness as the sea, it needs exceptional distance even to be seen. Only distance can confer the qualities that the painter requires. Even the summit, when finally reached, becomes quite invisible again - having existence only as a prospect.

Distant mountains with roads and paths leading towards them serve in paintings to represent the future, or open a place of speculation coloured by thoughts of time.
As a final backdrop, coloured palest blue or grey, vague and thus suggestive, painted mountains represent surely, if not hope, then with the mild persuasion of light cool colour

any ideal or fearful possibility that we can envisage there. Frequently in the staged paintings of Claude Lorraine and Poussin, the mountain's presence dignifies the human events of the foreground by giving perspective and context, a feeling of time and grand rootedness looking down dispassionately on the brief pastimes of the everyday.

Although many of the works described in this book have a topographic, descriptive purpose, the vastness of a view and the scale of a mountain must throw some colouring of innate memory or meaning that enhances their significance. Here we find many great figures of British art such as Richard Wilson, JMW Turner, John Varley, Paul Sandby, John Piper, Augustus John, Kyffin Williams. Their names alone are enough to remind us how this subject can inspire work of exceptional power and vision.

In the bardic tradition it is said that whoever who sleeps alone, high on the summit of Cader Idris, far above the bottomless lake of Llyn y Cau, wakes either as a madman or a poet.

Cader or Cadair, the chair, is said to be named after the mythological giant Idris, who surely also sought inspiration sitting on the vast mountain gazing up each night at the stars. Astronomer, philosopher and poet, he has all the ideal attributes of an artist dreaming of painting.

Christopher Le Brun PRA
President of the Royal Academy of Arts, London
October 2014

Edward Pugh, A Visit to Cader Idris, *aquatint, 11 x 14, in Edward Pugh,* Cambria Depicta, *London, 1816, p.206*

Preface

The aim of this book is to reveal the rich diversity of drawings, watercolours, prints and paintings that have been made of the mountains of Snowdonia over the past 250 years. It covers a wide range of artists and their works. The choice of images is based on their historical importance or contribution and in some cases it is a personal choice. Each of the nine viewpoint chapters has a short introductory essay followed by visual examples at each location. The individual artists' entries include a biography and a separate description of the illustrated work. There are 48 artists represented and over 70 full colour reproductions. Many are reproduced here for the first time. This book is a comprehensive survey of Snowdonia's mountain landscape art and it provides both a visual overview and an historical narrative.

This publication is the result of many years of involvement with Snowdonia and its mountain landscape. As an artist I have made drawings and paintings of this landscape since the mid 1980s. This interest led me to explore the visual history of Snowdonia along with research into the aesthetics artists used to represent it. This process led to a PhD from Aberystwyth University in 2002. Since then I have continued to investigate the subject and this book is the culmination of this journey.

All landscape paintings are an artificial construction. They are the result of a complex interchange between perceived reality and the created reality of art. Successful landscape paintings possess a degree of imagination that gives a greater life to the subject than it otherwise would have. This imaginative aspect can be seen in Richard Wilson's two significant paintings of Snowdon and Cader Idris particularly in the way in which the reality of the view is changed and transformed for the benefit of the spectator.

I have examined these issues initially by looking at both Snowdon and Cader Idris from a painter's point of view. As an artis, viewpoints become important as they predetermine the visual outcome from the start. Hence my involvement with mountain aesthetics and compositional formula that all played such an important role in the depiction of Snowdonia.

This book also includes a selection of quotes from the extensive travel literature along with a bibliography. I hope readers will enjoy discovering the range of pictures that artists have made to portray the mountains of Snowdonia from their first representation in the mid eighteenth century through to the present day.

PB

Acknowledgements

I would like to thank Myrddin ap Dafydd of Gwasg Carreg Gwalch for recognising the book's potential and for his belief in the importance of the subject matter. His support for the project from the start has been extremely reassuring to me.

I would also like to thank my first editor, Jen Llywelyn, for all her editorial support and advice given to me over many months as the book emerged from nothing to something. Thanks also to my second editor, Alun Gibbard, who has contributed his editorial expertise to the final stages of the book. Also special thanks to all the staff at Gwasg Carreg Gwalch for their publishing expertise.

My wife, Jenny who has coped with the everyday angst and frustrations of a developing text over the two years of research; editing my writing, collecting all the museum images and keeping accurate records of this process. This support has been invaluable to the development of the whole project.

A special debt of gratitude goes to Christopher Le Brun who made time to write the foreword while preparing for an exhibition of new paintings in New York along with his many duties as President of the Royal Academy of Arts.

I would also like to thank the artist Kevan Hopson, for his many suggestions and observations on contemporary art practice in Wales. In this context I would also like to thank the painter, David Woodford for his advice and support.

The artists: Pete Davis. Russell Gilder, Kevan Hopson, Robert Newell, David Tress, Matthew Wood and David Woodford all supplied information and images of the selected works.

Patrick and Claire Mansel Lewis of Stradey Castle, Llanelli for their help and information concerning his great grandfather, the artist Charles William Mansel Lewis and for arranging access for the photographer, Dan Staveley, to take photographs in situ.

Thanks are due to Richard Bishop Photography who photographed the majority of the pictures that were not in public collections. To Malcolm Payne of Colourfast Imaging for additional photography and for colour matching digital images to the original works.

To Alistair Crawford, Professor Emeritus, former head of the School of Art, Aberystwyth University, who was my Doctorate supervisor, a big thank you for all your continued support and advice.

Many thanks to my friend, the artist and photographer, John Myers who was always on hand to discuss issues pertinent to the development of ideas that subsequently became the book. I greatly benefitted from his support and encouragement.

All the museum pictures have been secured with the help of the staff concerned. To them all I offer my thanks. In some instances new photography was required and I am grateful to everyone who enabled this to happen with all the extra work involved. Special thanks to Nathan Pendlebury and his colleagues at the Walker Art Gallery who arranged for a painting in storage to be moved and unframed so it could be photographed specially for the book.

A number of copyright owners have given permission to publish works without a copyright fee. They are Pat Cross (plate 37), Ruth Lambert (plate 22), Clarissa Lewis (plate 54), Lesley Prendergast (plate 56) and Malka Holmes (plate 63).

Finally to my daughters, Izzy and Katie, who took an interest in the book's progress and provided encouragement at all times. I offer my grateful thanks.

Introduction

Snowdonia became a subject for landscape artists comparatively early. Pictorial and written records of visits date from the middle of the eighteenth century. It was a combination of factors that made this region a favoured location for both artists and visitors.

In the mid 1760s the Welsh-born landscape painter Richard Wilson (1713–1782) produced two oil paintings that highlighted the importance of the region. These two oils depicted Snowdon and Cader Idris. These paintings were commissioned by Welsh landowners and they show a landscape that represented their interests and promoted the idea of a Welsh idyll. In these paintings of Snowdonia's highest mountains Wilson has used a classical compositional formula brought back from his time in Italy. In 1775 a set of six large engraved prints were issued by John Boydell (1719–1804) with titles in both English and French. The set consists of three images of south Wales, *The Great Bridge over the Taaffe, Pembroke Town and Castle,* and *Kilgaran,* and three images of north Wales, *Caernarvon Castle, Snowdon and Cader Idris.* The publication of Snowdon and Cader Idris in print form greatly enhanced their pictorial status and this certainly helped to establish the mountain scenery of Snowdonia as a desirable commodity. They also introduced the idea of mountain scenery to a new audience of both artists and visitors. It was now worthwhile to make the journey to Snowdonia and see the mountain landscape for real.

The antiquary Thomas Pennant (1726–1798) did much to promote Snowdonia with his illustrated book *A Tour in Wales*, published in its finished two volume state in 1784. It contained a section titled *The Journey to Snowdon* (1781) in which a number of mountain views were drawn and engraved by the Welsh artist Moses Griffith (1747–1819). Many of these views established viewpoints that visitors could visit on their usually short tours to the region. These include Pont Aberglaslyn and the view of Snowdon from Capel Curig, both of which were visited by J. M. W. Turner (1775–1851) on his tours to north Wales in 1798 and 1799. As well as referring the reader to the engraved prints of both Snowdon and Cader Idris by Wilson, Pennant promotes the various sets of aquatints that Paul Sandby (1731–1809) issued in the late 1770s. These views of Snowdonia's mountain scenery were derived from his 1771 tour made with the Welsh landowner Sir Watkin Williams Wynn (1749–1789).

Other contributing factors include the arrival of William Gilpin's (1724–1804) picturesque aesthetic that was well established by 1800. Here was a great incentive for those artists who chose to work and explore its tripartite pictorial formula to visit sites in north Wales, such as Pont Aberglaslyn, which perfectly met their visual requirements.

The building of inns and hotels, along with the road improvements, made access to the most dramatic and rugged scenery possible. The A5, the former coach road, runs through the Nant Ffrancon pass which is one of the most desolate and mountainous parts of north Wales. Artists like the young J. M. W. Turner and many others were touring north Wales at the end of the eighteenth century because the Napoleonic wars had put a stop to travel to the Alps and Italy. This restriction on travel started in the 1790s and lasted intermittently to 1815, greatly adding to the popularity of north Wales for those artists and tourists seeking the excitement of exploring mountain scenery.

By the end of the eighteenth century Snowdonia was attracting a large number of artists, many of whom were part of the Romantic Movement. They were all looking for that aspect of mountain scenery that most suited their way of working and the aesthetics they wished to apply to their works. Snowdonia could satisfy the earlier need for a classical treatment of space comprising a number of recessional planes, a method that suited a vista to distant mountains, such as at Capel Curig with its distant view of Snowdon. The topographical treatment of accurate detail and the recording of reality was already a well established pictorial method. This was the aesthetic commonly used at the Nant Peris viewpoint towards Snowdon with Dolbadarn castle seen in the immediate foreground. The picturesque became the preferred aesthetic used by artists at Pont Aberglaslyn from the late eighteenth century through to the middle of the nineteenth. The sublime as a mode of vision was not applied by artists to the mountains of Snowdonia until the 1830s. It is characterised by a lack of recessional space and was applied to locations such as those found at Llyn Idwal and in the nearby mountains such as Tryfan above the Nant Ffrancon pass.

In Snowdonia artists could find and use the visual structures and methods they were familiar with and apply them to a viewpoint that met their needs and requirements. By about 1800, an increasingly large number of published tour journals and guidebooks led to an expanding number of artists and visitors making their own journeys into the mountains of Snowdonia. The first two decades of the nineteenth century saw many artists making tours, recording in sketchbooks and working up finished exhibition pieces in both watercolour and oil. These works could be

Fig. 1 Frontispiece to Journey to Snowdon

exhibited and sold in the new exhibition societies and at the Royal Academy in London which was again accepting landscape pictures. This was partly due to watercolour societies' acceptance of the landscape genre and the Academy's need to compete with them.

As the century progressed the demand for north Wales subjects continued and artists such as David Cox (1783–1859) became known for their views of Welsh scenery. A number of late Victorian painters also produced large scale oil paintings for the London market. By the twentieth century the area was still attracting artists such as James Dickson Innes (1887–1914) and Augustus John (1878–1961) and later John Piper (1903–1992).

The post-war period has seen a resurgence of interest in Snowdonia and its mountains as a subject for art. This period saw paintings of Snowdonia by Kyffin Williams (1918-2006) and Peter Prendergast (1946-2007), who both made a significant contribution to its continuing visual history. The contemporary interest in painting the mountains of north Wales continues and will, in time, add further to the pictorial history of Snowdonia.

Thomas Pennant on his extensive travels in north Wales:

My frequent journeys through them render me a tolerable master of their topography.
Thomas Pennant, A Tour in Wales, vol. 1, London, 1784, advertisement, p.2.

ONE
A View in Nant Peris: A Topographical Viewpoint

This viewpoint was reproduced by Thomas Pennant (1728–1798) in his book, *A Tour in Wales* (1784) and illustrates the view of Llanberis Lake and Dolbadarn Castle with Snowdon beyond. It was engraved from a watercolour drawn by the Welsh topographical artist Moses Griffith (1747–1819). At this location, although Snowdon can be seen at the head of the Llanberis Pass, the castle is often the dominant feature, with the view of Snowdon forming a backdrop rather than the main subject. An early view of the castle was recorded in an engraving by N. and S. Buck published in 1742.

A topographical treatment was particularly suited for recording architectural subjects such as houses and castles. In landscape painting it presents a clear and precise rendering of the scene. Because the main pictorial focus at this location is usually the castle tower in the foreground, it is best represented using a topographical format. The Royal Academy has an unbroken record of annual summer exhibitions since 1769. Twenty works with Dolbadarn Castle in the title were exhibited there in the years up until 1876, when the mountains themselves became a more favoured subject. In the twentieth century it became a popular subject in photography thereby retaining its link with the topographical tradition. Today it is still popular in its photographic form and is often used in the promotional literatures associated with north Wales.

Another approach to this subject especially in the eighteenth century was to represent the castle in a classical light reminiscent of Italy. The Welsh artist Richard Wilson (1713–1782) painted several oils of this subject in the early 1760s appropriating the status that the castle possessed as a significant historical site. The paintings are not topographical as they do not present a factual account of place, rather they are Italianate composites of idealised beauty depicted in a clear classical light. A version of this subject dating from 1762-4 is in the National Museum of Wales, Cardiff.

Joseph Mallord William Turner (1775–1851) visited this location on his 1798 and 1799 sketching tours to north Wales. In his Dolbadarn sketchbook of 1799 he made various studies, many of these are based on the same viewpoint used by Moses Griffith to illustrated Pennant's book. The sketches Turner produced on this visit were worked up for his Royal Academy oil painting *Dolbadarn Castle* with the castle depicted in a classical light. This work of 1800 was exhibited in 1802 as his diploma work and is in the Academy's collection. A finished oil study of the same subject is in the collection of the National Library of Wales.

> Pennant's description of the view of Dolbadarn castle and Snowdon:
>
> *This is a very picturesque vale, bounded by the base of Snowdon, Cefn Cum Gafr, the two Glyders, and two Llyders, each of them first rate mountains... On the loftiest part over one of the lakes, stand the remains of Castell Dolbadarn, consisting of a round tower, and a few fragments of walls.*
>
> Thomas Pennant, A Tour in Wales, vol. 2., London, 1784, p.165.

PLATES 1-6

1

Paul Sandby, *Snowdon in Caernarvonshire*, 1781 (first published 1779), engraving, 13.2 x 18.3, private collection

Paul Sandby (1730–1809) was primarily a topographical watercolour artist and a pioneer of aquatint, a new method of reproducing watercolours in print form. He appears largely self-taught, but probably had some instruction from his older brother Thomas Sandby (1723–1798). In 1747 he secured a position at the Board of Ordnance as a military draughtsman and map-maker. As a result of his military duties in the highlands of Scotland he began to make topographical transcriptions of actual landscape views. Along with his brother Thomas, he was part of the original group of twenty artists who formed the Royal Academy with the full support of King George III in December 1768. Also in 1768 he was appointed drawing master at the Royal Military Academy in Woolwich. His large topographical watercolours made at Windsor Great Park form an important group of works. His sets of aquatint prints, derived from his tours to both north and south Wales in the 1770s, did much to introduce Welsh landscape scenery and the picturesque aesthetic to a wider audience.

Snowdon in Caernarvonshire depicts a view towards Snowdon in a cameo with a decorative border framing the whole picture. This print was published by Boydell in *A Collection of One Hundred and Fifty Select Views in England, Wales, Scotland and Ireland* in 1781. The decorative border that frames the image was added by Boydell's engravers, a common practice on a reissued print. The added border contains a family group at bottom left and, on the right, a blind Welsh harpist is shown. Dolbadarn Castle is silhouetted on the right with Snowdon rising beyond the lake and castle. The overall image presents Snowdonia's highest mountain as a non-threatening accessible commodity. Paul Sandby was an early visitor to north Wales and is credited with making the first recorded tour in 1771. Whilst on this tour with Sir Watkin Williams Wynn the touring party made a detour to Dolbadarn Castle.

1. Paul Sandby, Snowdon in Caernarvonshire, *1781, (published 1779), engraving, 13.2 x 18.3, private collection*

2
Samuel H Grimm, *Dolbadarn Castle,* **engraving, 15.1 x 21, in Henry Penruddocke Wyndham,** *A Gentleman's Tour through Monmouthshire and Wales. Made in the months of June and July 1774, and in the months of June, July and August 1777.* **Salisbury, 1781, plate XIII**

Samuel Hieronymus Grimm (1733–1794) was a Swiss topographical artist who worked in a wide range of graphic media. Originally he was trained in oil painting in Bern but later specialised in watercolour, etching and monochrome wash drawings, covering a range of subjects from architecture to landscape views. Grimm spent time living and travelling in France until 1769, when he moved to England. He was based in Derbyshire in 1775 and was resident in London from 1778. Grimm travelled extensively around England and Wales and was employed as a professional artist to make visual records for a number of patrons. Sir Richard Kaye (1736–1809) employed the artist for two decades to make drawings of 'anything curious'. He accompanied Henry P Wyndham (1736–1819) on his second Welsh tour to make drawings to illustrate his travel book, published in 1781. The British Library has a large collection of his work.

In *Dolbadarn Castle* by Samuel H Grimm, reproduced as plate thirteen in Wyndham's travel book, we are presented with a topographically accurate interpretation of the location. The round tower of the castle on the right is the main focus of the composition, with mountains filling the remainder of the landscape. It is rendered in sharp detail with a pale sky that occupies about 50 per cent of the remaining picture area. In the foreground two figures can be seen herding cattle along the lake shore and all are shown silhouetted against the water. All the engraved plates in *A Gentleman's Tour through Monmouth and Wales* are topographical in nature and their realism, as in Pennant's more substantial *A Tour in Wales*, contributed to the visualisation of the scenery of north Wales.

2. Samuel H Grimm, Dolbadarn Castle, *engraving, 15.1 x 21, in Henry Penruddocke Wyndham,* A Gentleman's Tour through Monmouthshire and Wales. *Salisbury, 1781, plate XIII*

3
Moses Griffith, *A View in Nant Beris*, engraving, 12.6 x 18.4, in Thomas Pennant, *A Tour in Wales, The Journey to Snowdon*, vol. 2, London, 1784, plate VIII

Moses Griffith (1747–1819) was a Welsh topographical artist who was employed by the antiquary and naturalist Thomas Pennant (1726–1798) as a topographical draughtsman to make illustrations for his many books. Griffith was resident in north Wales, later living on the Pennant estate at Downing near Whitford in Flintshire. Griffith accompanied Pennant on many excursions and tours. Travelling mostly on horseback, he acted as a manservant as well as an artist. On these journeys Griffith made watercolour sketches that were later engraved to accompany Pennant's written narratives. Volume one of *A Tour in Wales* was published in 1778. It was followed by *The Journey to Snowdon* section in 1781. The complete two volume edition was published in 1784.

A View in Nant Beris was drawn under Pennant's direction and was engraved for *A Tour in Wales*. This illustration shows Llanberis Lake and Dolbadarn Castle with Snowdon beyond. In the immediate foreground two figures are walking by the lakeshore; one carrying a pair of oars and the other a bundle on his back. They are about to set out in the boat that is moored close to the foreshore. The composition consists of a series of recessional planes creating pictorial space. The whole landscape is portrayed in a sharp and clear focused light that is characteristic of this particular form of realism.

Pennant on Moses Griffith, the illustrator of A Tour in Wales:

The drawings marked MOSES GRIFFITH are the performances of a worthy servant whom I keep for that purpose. The candid will excuse any little imperfections they may find in them; as they are the work of an untaught genius, drawn from the most remote and obscure parts of North Wales.

Thomas Pennant, A Tour in Wales, vol. 1, London, 1784, advertisement p.4.

A View in Nant Peris

3. *Moses Griffith*, A View in Nant Beris, *engraving, 12.6 x 18.4, in Thomas Pennant,* A Tour in Wales, The Journey to Snowdon, *vol. 2, London, 1784, plate VIII*

4
Joseph Mallord William Turner, *Lake Llanberis and Dolbadarn Castle, with Snowdon Beyond,* **1799, gouache graphite and watercolour on paper, 55.7 x 76.5, Tate Britain**

Joseph Mallord William Turner (1775–1851) was one of Britain's most significant landscape painters of the nineteenth century. Based in London he was a student at the Academy Schools and was elected a full member of the Royal Academy in 1802. Prior to this date Turner made several tours to north Wales at a time when access to the continent was too dangerous due to the various disputes in Europe caused by the Napoleonic Wars. Turner visited Wales a number of times between 1792 and 1800. The visits to Snowdonia were made in 1798 and again in 1799. He was probably hoping for better weather on his second visit. He made many sketchbook drawings and monochrome wash studies at the Dolbadarn castle viewpoint previously drawn by Moses Griffith and published in Thomas Pennant's book, *A Tour in Wales* (1784). On these trips Turner took sketchbooks of various sizes and some larger sheets of paper carefully wrapped to protect them from the weather.

In this large watercolour by Turner, now titled *Lake Llanberis and Dolbadarn Castle with Snowdon Beyond*, we are presented with an expansive view across the lake towards a majestic-looking Snowdon. The viewpoint is some distance away from the castle, which is now reduced in size and is no longer the main focus of the picture. It is, however, placed on the golden section within the composition and acts as an axis point, and it also helps to establish a relative scale for the rest of the picture. Snowdon rises upwards at the head of the valley and is clear of the enveloping cloud that often obscured the mountain. There is no foreshore present and this compositional device suggests elements of the sublime, a device Turner would later use in his paintings of the Alps. Many visitors to this location took an excursion on the lake and maybe Turner also made such a trip. The reduced colour used in the work enabled Turner to work quickly with the aid of linear drawing as a guide for the rapidly executed tonal washes he applied to this work.

A View in Nant Peris 27

4. Joseph Mallord William Turner, Lake Llanberis and Dolbadarn Castle, with Snowdon Beyond. *1799, Gouache graphite and watercolour on paper, 55.7 x 76.5, Tate Britain*

5
Edmund Becker, *View of Dolbadarn Castle with Snowdon beyond*, 1808–12, wash drawing, 20 x 29, private collection

Edmund Becker (fl.1790–1812) (his dates are still unknown) made numerous wash drawings between 1790 and 1812. His monochrome wash drawings made on the spot on his travels have only recently been discovered and attributions reassessed. It is likely that more works will come to light in the future. It appears that Becker made wash drawings of castles and mountain landscapes in north Wales in 1806, 1808, 1811 and 1812. These drawings were originally in sketchbooks, now broken up. Many of these drawings are numbered so it is possible to piece together the tour itinerary. There is a sketchbook in the collection of the National Library of Wales that has an intriguing title: *Sketches after nature drawn in Mr and Mrs Becker's journey into north Wales and South Wales after their marriage*. This sketch book is dated 10th September 1812 and is inscribed in Becker's hand.

Dolbadarn Castle with Snowdon beyond was drawn on one of Becker's tours to north Wales and is probably from his visit in 1808. The sunlit castle is positioned in the centre of the composition with the mountains forming the backdrop to the castle. This visual structure adheres to William Gilpin's aesthetic of picturesque beauty consisting of three planes, foreground, middle distance and background. This formula was helpful for artists with limited time and visual experience as it enabled them to record a subject comprehensively on the spot. Becker's views can be seen as visual memoranda rather than interpretative views.

Some visitors took to a boat on the lake as recorded by William Bingley:

Seated as we were in the boat, nearly on a level with the surface of the water, the lake, on looking along its whole extent, had the appearance of being large and expansive. The mountains arranged in the most beautiful manner imaginable... Snowdon, with its deep and perpendicular precipice, and two summits, forms an immense mass of mountain; which constitutes the principal feature. The lake, the round tower of Dolbadarn, the distant vale and mountains, and, on the other side, the huge rock of Glyder Vawr, lend each its character to heighten the effect of the whole.

William Bingley, North Wales, 1814, p.143.

5. *Edmund Becker*, View of Dolbadarn Castle with Snowdon beyond, *1808–12, wash drawing, 20 x 29, private collection*

6
Thomas Creswick, *Dolbadarn Tower*, engraving, 9.7 x 14.5, in Thomas Roscoe, *Wanderings and Excursions in North Wales*, London, 1836, plate XIX

Thomas Creswick (1819–1869) was a landscape painter in both oil and watercolour. He was also commissioned to make illustrations for a number of publications and print portfolios. Creswick often painted outside and this gives an authenticity to his landscape views. He was resident in Birmingham where he was taught by John Vincent Barber (1788–1838) and then in 1828 moved to London. Creswick first exhibited at the Society of British Artists in 1827 and at the Royal Academy the following year, where he showed two views of north Wales. In all, he exhibited over a hundred works at the Academy. He was elected to the Royal Academy as an associate in 1842, and RA in 1851. Perhaps his best known painting is his oil titled *Lands End, Cornwall* painted in 1842 and exhibited at the British Institution in 1843, where it won that year's prize. It depicts a view of the Atlantic from a high vantage point. Its rich colour and meticulously observed detail anticipates the outdoor landscapes of the Pre-Raphaelite movement. This work is in the collection of the Victoria and Albert Museum, London.

This engraved view of Dolbadarn Castle was published in Thomas Roscoe's (1791–1871) travel guide, *Wanderings and Excursions in North Wales* published in 1836. Creswick was one of the group of artists (which also included David Cox) commissioned to illustrate the viewpoints selected by Roscoe, whose text they accompanied. This image was engraved by William Radclyffe (1780–1855) and is of the finest quality. In this view Creswick has placed the castle nearer the centre of the composition and he has shown two figures in a boat staring directly out of the picture at the viewer. Roscoe cited Pennant on the history of the castle and then records the experience of seeing the view bathed in moonlight. He wrote, 'It was soon moonlight and I beheld a prospect mirrored in the silvery waters softer and more serenely fair than is seen in the glare of the day.'[1] *Dolbadarn Tower* illustrates a moonlight scene with Roscoe presumably the figure sitting on the left in the boat. Thomas Roscoe also published a companion volume on south Wales in 1837. It followed the same format and was illustrated by a range of artists, again including Creswick.

A View in Nant Peris

6. *Thomas Creswick,* Dolbadarn Tower, *engraving, 9.7 x 14.5, in Thomas Roscoe,* Wanderings and Excursions in North Wales, *London, 1836, plate XIX*

TWO
Snowdon from Capel Curig: A Classical Viewpoint

Snowdon as seen from Capel Curig is one of the finest views in Britain. This much photographed vista has been used extensively in the promotional literature of north Wales and Snowdonia. Colour postcards, calendars, picture books and reproduction prints all have contained this image in photographic form. The compositional formula used for this vista is classical; a carefully balanced and controlled sequence of recessional planes through which the eye is led. This concept was used extensively by landscape artists working in Italy in the seventeenth century, such as Nicholas Poussin (1593–1665) and it was first applied to the representation of Snowdon in the mid eighteenth century. This visual sequence runs from foreground to the middle distance and then through to the background where the whole panorama of Snowdon fills the distant horizon.

This viewpoint is close to the amenities of Capel Curig, which provide a degree of security and protection for those contemplating the vista towards Snowdon. The view contains both mountain and lake, two powerful landscape features of Snowdonia. Sometimes Snowdon is seen reflected on the flat surface of the water to give a mirror-like effect, and this characteristic is often present when lake Mymbyr occupies the immediate foreground. Another feature is that the summit of Snowdon is often shown obscured by cloud, and other peaks are sometimes hidden as well. This gives the impression that the mountains are significantly higher than they really are. This viewpoint also has certain features of topography that reminded visitors and travellers of Alpine scenery.

Thomas Pennant highlighted this aspect of the location when he wrote, 'Snowdon and his many sons, *Crib Goch, Crib-Y-Distill, Lliwedd-Yr-Arran,* and many others, here burst at once full in view, and make this far the finest approach to our boasted Alps'.[2]

Pennant's *A Tour in Wales* was published in 1784. It contained an engraving of the view of Snowdon from Capel Curig by Moses Griffith. This image, along with Griffith's, *A View in Nant Beris*, which depicts the view towards Snowdon from Dolbadarn Castle, would have been seen by Philippe Jacques de Loutherbourg (1740–1812) and quite possibly gave him his cue for the two oil paintings exhibited at the Royal Academy in 1787. The artist had made a tour to north Wales the previous year and both paintings were exhibition pieces and would have enhanced

Snowdonia's landscape status when they were exhibited in London.

This subject became popular from the late seventeen-eighties onwards particularly among those artists, like John Varley (1778–1842), who preferred to use a classical formula for their pictures. Although this viewpoint provided an ideal structure for such a treatment there are examples where the view became obscured due to the weather, allowing for a sublime treatment to come to the fore.

Some artists treated the view in a straightforward topographical manner or variations of approaches that could be applied to this expansive panorama of Snowdon. During the nineteenth century the view was still represented but it fell out of favour by the twentieth century as artists ceased to construct paintings using the classical model. However its popularity in photographic form continues to the present day.

William Bingley on improvements at Capel Curig in 1801:

Those tourists who, like myself, have visited this vale some years ago, when the only place of public accommodation was a mean pot-house ... will be able with some justice to appreciate the spirited conduct, and truly patriotic exertions of the noble proprietor, who has not only constructed for them an inn, but who was the first to make this part of the country passable in carriages.

William Bingley, North Wales, 1814, p.293.

PLATES 7-12

7

Philippe Jacques de Loutherbourg, *Snowdon from Capel Curig, a morning*, 1787, oil on canvas, 134.5 x 200, Yale Center for British Art, Paul Mellon Collection

Philippe Jacques de Loutherbourg (1740–1812) was a French artist who was based in London from 1771 onwards working as a landscape painter and stage set designer for theatres such as the Garrick. He invented the Eidophusikon, an early method of making small-scale projections using mirrors and other optical devices. This was first opened to the public in 1781. He made an excursion to Derbyshire in 1778 primarily to make preparatory sketches for stage sets for a pantomime production in Drury Lane. In 1783 de Loutherbourg made a 'picturesque tour' of Derbyshire and the Lake District from which a series of landscapes in oil were made. De Loutherbourg visited Wales in 1786 to make landscape studies influenced by William Gilpin's example and these include a wide range of subjects ranging from picturesque ruins such as Tintern Abbey to studies of castles such as Conwy and Harlech along with views of mountain scenery. Two paintings of Snowdon, the result of this tour, were exhibited at the Royal Academy the following year. These were, *View of Snowdon, from Llyn Beris lake, with the castle of Dolbardon*, and *View of Snowdon from Capel Curig, a morning*. Sixty-nine studies from this Welsh tour are in the collection of the National Library of Wales.

In this oil painting of 1787 de Loutherbourg presents a view of Snowdon from Capel Curig bathed in an early morning light reminiscent of Italy, as seen in Richard Wilson's earlier painting. Like Wilson, de Loutherbourg has chosen a classical construction for his view of the Snowdon panorama. Painted in his London studio, this large work was conceived as an exhibition piece and was exhibited at the Royal Academy in 1787.

In *Snowdon from Capel Curig, a morning*, the topographical, the classical and the picturesque all combine into one composition. The landscape is accurately represented and any exaggerations of form, for example, in the Snowdon massif itself, only reinforces and adds to its visual identity. De Loutherbourg has shown the small footbridge set on the golden mean which acts as a compositional anchor for the eye and a point of human accessibility, a reality that counterbalances the exaggerations of the mountain forms. A group of buildings can be seen on the extreme right of the painting; they include stables for the increasing through traffic on the route from Betws-y-Coed to Bangor. A small church and some travellers give scale to the view. On the left, a man on a horse is shown pulling a sledge along the dirt road. This was a popular method of moving bulk before the road improvements that would shortly transform the area's communications.

In the centre foreground is a large rock upon which the artist has inscribed his name and the date 1787, perhaps a theatrical gesture he could not resist!

7. Philippe Jacques de Loutherbourg, Snowdon from Capel Curig, a morning, *1787, oil on canvas, 134.5 x 200, Yale Center for British Art, Paul Mellon Collection*

8
Moses Griffith, *The Summit of Snowdon from Capel Cerig*, engraving, 12.2 x 19, in Thomas Pennant, *A Tour in Wales, The Journey to Snowdon*, vol. 2, London, 1784, plate VII

Moses Griffith (1747–1819) was a topographical watercolour artist and engraver. He was largely self-taught, but the naturalist Thomas Pennant (1726–1798) recognised his talent from about 1769 onwards and under his direction encouraged him to study drawing and engraving. Pennant subsequently employed Griffith to make watercolour drawings to illustrate his many publications. Many of these pictures were engraved by Griffith and were used to illustrated Pennant's books. He also produced topographical views of country houses, churches and views of Welsh scenery. Following the death of Thomas Pennant in 1798 he was engaged by his son David Pennant, and between 1805 and 1813 he made over 200 watercolours of Wales.

The summit of Snowdon from Capel Cerig is one the first published images for this viewpoint towards Snowdon. In its engraved form it was seen by many artists and tourists about to visit Snowdonia as they used the *Journey to Snowdon* (1781) section of Pennant's *A Tour in Wales*, as their guide. This view by Griffith accompanies the written description of the view by Pennant. Although topographical in its representation it does retain compositional elements of the classical, such as the tree on the left which fills the picture space from top to bottom. Another feature is the deep recessional space that is a characteristic feature of this view of Snowdon. There is plenty of human activity present, a busy hay harvest is taking place and laden drays are shown along with horses and men carrying hay. These figures are depicted along the bottom edge of the frame almost as a frieze which was a pictorial convention of the day.

View of Snowdon from the hotel at Capel Curig:

This little village, whose chief structure is the large and capital hotel, where we now were, stands in a spot exceedingly convenient for some of the finest scenery of Snowdonia, and from which three vallies of distinct character radiate.

G J Freeman, Sketches in Wales, London, 1826, p.117.

Snowdon from Capel Curig 37

8. *Moses Griffith,* The Summit of Snowdon from Capel Cerig, *engraving, 12.2 x 19, in Thomas Pennant,* A Tour in Wales, The Journey to Snowdon, *vol. 2, London, 1784, plate VII*

9
Joseph Mallord William Turner, *View from Capel Curig towards Snowdon, the mountains under cloud*, 1798, pencil and watercolour on paper, 22.5 x 33.2, Tate Britain

J. M. W. Turner (1775–1851) was one of Britain's most significant landscape painters, excelling in both watercolour and oil. He became a student at the Royal Academy Schools in 1789. In 1796 Turner exhibited his first oil painting at the Academy. During this decade he began making tours through Britain including five tours to Wales between 1792 and 1799. These excursions were made mostly in the summer months and the drawings and watercolour studies formed the source material for oil paintings made during the winter months in London. Turner's oil painting *Dolbadarn Castle*, completed in 1800, was his 1802 diploma picture for the Royal Academy, and was based on studies made at the site in 1799 during his last tour to north Wales. Turner's long and successful artistic career continued to his death and he bequeathed a large body of work to the nation. The Turner Bequest is housed in Tate Britain.

View from Capel Curig towards Snowdon, the mountains under cloud was drawn on the spot in 1798. This study is in Turner's Hereford Court sketchbook, which contains a number of other studies of mountain scenery. These include a series of rain-spattered watercolours made on Cader Idris when Turner was exploring the site of Richard Wilson's view of the mountain painted in 1765. The sketchbook begins in south Wales and then features views in north Wales. Many of Turner's views of Snowdonia are from the same locations highlighted in Thomas Pennant's *A Tour in Wales*. In this quickly executed study we can appreciate Turner's immediate response to the view. Turner has shown Snowdon's summit obscured by cloud. This was a particular feature of the location.

9. Joseph Mallord William Turner, View from Capel Curig towards Snowdon, the mountains under cloud, *1798, pencil and watercolour on paper, 22.5 x 33.2, Tate Britain*

10
John Varley, *Snowdon from Capel Curig*, 1805–1810, unfinished watercolour, 35.5 x 45.5, Victoria and Albert Museum, London

John Varley (1778–1842) was a London-based professional watercolour artist, mostly of landscape views. He visited north Wales in 1799 with the landscape artist George Arnold (1763–1841). He went again in 1800. In 1802 he toured Snowdonia with his younger brother Cornelius, and they met up with fellow artists Joshua Cristall (1768–1847), William Havell (1782–1857) and the architect Thomas Webster (1772–1844) who were also visiting north Wales. This was Varley's last documented tour to north Wales although many of his Welsh subjects were made after this date. He exhibited 739 works at the Old Water Colour Society and forty-one at the Royal Academy. Varley's views of north Wales became a prominent feature of the London exhibitions. Many of these were re-workings of popular subjects such as his views of Snowdon.

This watercolour was made some years after Varley's last visit to Snowdonia. In its unfinished state we can see the artist's working methods. The structural elements are carefully drawn in pencil; the contour lines drawn lightly, so as not to intrude into the watercolour washes. The distant mountain forms in shadow are shown in cold blue-grey washes, emphasising their solidity. The view is presented in a classical guise similar to that used in De Loutherbourg's earlier picture of 1787, but Varley has shown the mountains more truthfully, with less exaggeration of shape than in De Loutherbourg's picture. A group of Italianate trees on the right emphasises the classical over the objective and this restricts the realism of the scene, contributing to the overall artificial look of the picture. Varley, in *Snowdon from Capel Curig* is making a composite picture. A number of visual ingredients such as mountain, wood, lake and river are all combined to satisfy a particular taste. There are a large number of versions of this subject catering for his many patrons' varying tastes.

10. John Varley, Snowdon from Capel Curig, *c. 1805-10, unfinished watercolour, 35.5 x 45.5, Victoria and Albert Museum, London*

11
Edward Pugh, *North-East View of Snowdon*, 1813, aquatint print, 15 x 19.8, in Edward Pugh, *Cambria Depicta: A Tour through North Wales Illustrated with Picturesque Views By a Native Artist*, London, 1816, p. 114

Edward Pugh (1763–1813) was a Welsh-speaking travel writer and watercolour artist. He was born at Ruthin in north Wales but was chiefly resident in London. Here he produced miniaturist works and exhibited at the Royal Academy. While in London he met John Boydell (1719–1804) the print publisher. it was Boydell who suggested to Pugh the original idea for an illustrated book on north Wales. He returned to Ruthin in 1800 and started travelling around north Wales making watercolour drawings and notes for his illustrated guide, *Cambria Depicta*. This volume contains seventy-one aquatinted plates, including ten of mountain scenery. Interestingly, Pugh gave his own titles to the reproduced prints even when they were well-known under other names. *Cambria Depicta* was published in 1816 three years after Pugh's death.

In Edward Pugh's aquatint *North-East View of Snowdon* there is no indication in the title that it is a view from Capel Curig. Any mention of Capel Curig would have identified the location, therefore diminishing Pugh's assertions on originality. This image adheres to the compositional structures and chiaroscuro arrangements found in de Loutherbourg's earlier painting of the view. The lake in Pugh's version is shown in a light tone, as it is in de Loutherbourg's picture. Pugh has emphasised the cloud-obscured peaks, a characteristic of the location, and a feature observed by Moses Griffith in his engraved picture published in 1784. In this composition Pugh has focused on the mountain panorama that frames the vista. The awkwardly-placed cottage on the left, with smoke emerging from the chimney, adds a sense of reality to the scene. Pugh, on his visit to Capel Curig, stayed at the newly refurbished inn that was situated very close to the viewpoint.

Snowdon from Capel Curig

11. Edward Pugh, North-East View of Snowdon, *1813, aquatint print, 15 x 19.8, in Edward Pugh,* Cambria Depicta, *London, 1816, p.114*

12
George Grainger Smith, *Snowdon from Capel Curig*, 1939, oil on board, 64.2 x 76.8, Walker Art Gallery, National Museums Liverpool

George Grainger Smith (1892–1961) was a landscape painter in both watercolour and oil. He was also a printmaker specialising in dry point etching. Grainger Smith was born in Hull and studied at the Liverpool School of Art. He lived in Wallasey on Merseyside, and was a member of the Liverpool Academy of Arts and an art teacher at the Liverpool College. He also exhibited at the Royal Academy and at other regional galleries. Grainger Smith was a member of the Royal Cambrian Academy and was its President in 1961. His paintings are in a number of private and public collections.

Snowdon from Capel Curig conforms to the established visual identity associated with this view towards Snowdon. The classical structure of the site is retained in this naturalistic vision of the vista. The footbridge and the building, formally the Royal Hotel, are depicted. It is a reassuring scene of pastoral tranquillity complete with grazing sheep in the foreground, painted in 1939 as the world prepared for war. The treatment of light conforms to the normal pattern of light and dark associated with this view. The distant mountain mass is shown in a natural light and it, along with the sky, is the lightest tone in the picture. The sky consists of groups of thin clouds forming recessional bands that reinforce the classically grand space the artist has constructed. This painting by Grainger Smith adheres to a compositional formula first established by de Loutherbourg in 1787.

12. George Grainger Smith, Snowdon from Capel Curig, *1939, oil on board, 64.2 x 76.8, Walker Art Gallery, Liverpool*

THREE
Views of Snowdon

The first significant painting of Snowdon was made by the Welsh born artist Richard Wilson (1713–1782) who had recently returned from an extended visit to Italy. He applied what he had learnt there to the landscape of Snowdonia. His view of Snowdon is seen from a distance and is bathed in an Italian light. *Snowdon from Llyn Nantlle* was originally purchased by the wealthy landowner William Vaughan (1707–1775), who was a member of the Cymmrodorion Society and its President from 1751 to 1775. The aim of the Society is to promote Welsh identity and culture. A version of this subject was exhibited in London at the Society of Artists exhibition in 1766 and it would have introduced the subject to a new audience. Later, it was issued as a print, the fifth one of a set of six by John Boydell in 1775, which greatly added to its popularity. Wilson's painting and associated prints introduced the idea that Wales and its mountain scenery might be worth a visit.

When Thomas Pennant (1726–1798) published the first definitive guide book on north Wales, *A Tour in Wales* in 1784, he did not illustrate Wilson's view of Snowdon. Instead, he referred the reader to the published engraving of Wilson's painting. Paul Sandby (1730–1809) issued three sets of Welsh aquatint prints in editions of twelve prints per set, during the second half of the 1770s. A number of these prints are views of Snowdonia's mountain scenery and were promoted and highlighted by Pennant in his book. All this activity contributed to the promotion of north Wales and its attraction to visitors and artists alike.

Snowdon itself (the highest mountain in Wales at 1085m), became increasingly accessible as the roads were improved. Thomas Telford's new wide road to Holyhead through the heart of Snowdonia was finally completed in 1826. There followed an expansion of available accommodation at inns and newly-constructed hotels, and making a tour to north Wales became a fashion. By the beginning of the nineteenth century the picturesque tour in north Wales had become highly popular.

As the nineteenth century progressed, Wilson's original viewpoint towards Snowdon was little used. A number of other viewpoints became established and many of these satisfied the requirements of a sublime aesthetic. This often resulted in a much closer view of the mountain than the classical structure applied by Wilson in his painting. As the century turned into the twentieth, artists increasingly sought out their own individual responses to Snowdon and its adjacent mountain scenery.

Viewpoint for Richard Wilson's Snowdon from Llyn Nantlle described by Pennant:

It is from this spot that MR. WILSON has favoured us with a view as magnificent as it is faithful. Few are sensible of this as few visit the spot.

Thomas Pennant, A Tour in Wales, vol.2., London, 1784, p.188.

PLATES 13-22

13
Richard Wilson, *Snowdon*, c. 1764-5. graphite on paper, 20.6 x 32.1, Huntington Library, San Marino, California, USA

14
Richard Wilson, *Snowdon from Llyn Nantlle*, 1765-6, oil on canvas, 101.6 x 127, Walker Art Gallery, Liverpool

Richard Wilson (1713–1782) was a professional portrait and landscape painter in oils. He came from Penegoes, near Machynlleth in mid Wales, where his father was a clergyman. Here he received a good classical education. Wilson was related on his mother's side to the Vaughans and the Wynns of Wynnstay. He studied in London and then in Italy from 1750 to 1757. Wilson was based in Rome where, influenced by the classical French painters, he began to paint landscapes of his own. He painted views of the campagna with its ruined architectural features such as temples and statues. These structures formed an integral part of the imaginative element in the compositional formula that he applied to these paintings of the Roman countryside. On his return to London he painted landscapes that were influenced by his time in Italy. This classical concept was ideally suited for the portrayal of the British country house estates, depicted by Wilson as if they were in Italy. A founder member of the Royal Academy in 1768, he returned to live in Wales in 1781. There are several versions of Wilson's paintings of Snowdon and Cader Idris in other collections and some are still untraced. There is another version of *Snowdon from Llyn Nantlle* in the Castle Museum, Nottingham.

Snowdon is a preliminary pencil drawing for Wilson's oil painting, *Snowdon from Llyn Nantlle*. Drawn on location, it depicts the main topographical features of the landscape vista towards Snowdon. Many of these features were retained in the final painting.

In *Snowdon from Llyn Nantlle* (1765) Wilson has chosen to represent an image of the mountain based upon a natural vista that conveniently fitted the classical model. The Italian light is now cast onto a Welsh mountain landscape and Snowdon appears as if it is situated in the campagna in Italy. The deep areas of shadow around the foreground lakes indicate that an early morning scene is shown. Wilson has painted a contemporary landscape as well as an ideal one.

On the lower lake, two boats with people can be seen and, at the head of the lake, a single figure in a boat. On the second lake there are a further six boats, although now they appear as mere specks in the distance. Above this area a pall of smoke ascends gently, suggesting a workaday activity taking place in the landscape. In the immediate foreground close to the lake shore are three figures in a classical guise. They may not be fishing as is often suggested. The two male figures are local to this landscape and are busy entertaining their lady visitor with a unique curiosity of the location. This was the so-called floating island, a feature of the lake and an entertaining sight to be shown to visitors. A piece of former bank had broken free from the lake side, a feature observed by Pennant in *A Tour in Wales*. He stated 'it frequently is set in motion by the wind; often joins its native banks... and cattle are frequently surprised on it.'[3]

13. Richard Wilson, Snowdon, *c. 1764-5. graphite on paper, 20.6 x 32.1, Huntington Library, San Marino, California, USA*

14. Richard Wilson, Snowdon from Llyn Nantlle, *1765-6, oil on canvas, 101.6 x 127, Walker Art Gallery, Liverpool*

15
John Warwick Smith, *An Ascent of Snowdon*, 1790, watercolour over graphite on paper, 13.8 x 20.8, British Museum

John Warwick Smith (1749–1831) was primarily a watercolour painter who produced his most accomplished work while in Italy between 1776 and 1781 under the patronage of George Greville, 2nd Earl of Warwick. He inserted the name Warwick to differentiate himself from others with the same name. He studied with Sawrey Gilpin (1733–1807) a painter of equine subjects. After his time in Italy he supplied drawings for various publications including six views for Middiman's *Select Views in Great Britain* (1784-5). His first visit to Wales was made in 1784 and he made frequent visits thereafter, the last in 1806. In these tours Smith sought out both picturesque and sublime locations for his landscape views. He also toured the Lake District in the early 1790s at a time when the pursuit of the Picturesque was the new fashion. Many of his views were published in a variety of print sets and tour books such as William Sotheby's *Tour through Parts of Wales* published in 1794. From 1797 he was resident in London.

In the watercolour *An Ascent of Snowdon* John Warwick Smith shows a touring party struggling up a steep slope towards the summit of Snowdon. We see two people on horseback with another leading the way. This figure is most likely to have been hired as a guide and his local knowledge and awareness of the weather conditions would have been invaluable to the visiting party unfamiliar with the terrain. Smith has chosen a composition that emphasises the dramatic and dizzying heights reached by the party on the rugged and potentially dangerous mountain. The expansive vista beyond the figures is partly obscured by swirling clouds and this produces a sublime rather than a picturesque aesthetic. Smith has used local colour applied directly to the paper with little evidence of a drawn outline visible in the finished picture.

15. John Warwick Smith, An Ascent of Snowdon, *1790, watercolour over graphite on paper, 13.8 x 20.8, British Museum*

Changeable weather on Snowdon as observed by Bingley:

The summit of Snowdon is so frequently enveloped in clouds and mist... even when the state of the weather seems favourable, it will often become suddenly enveloped... Most persons, however, agree that the prospects are the more interesting, as they are more varied, when the clouds just cover the summit.

William Bingley, North Wales, London, 1814, p.167.

16
J. M. W. Turner, *Y Garn with Snowdon in the Distance, from above Llyn Nantlle*, 1799. gouache, graphite and watercolour on paper, 55.7 x 76.8, Tate Britain

Joseph Mallord William Turner (1775–1851) was a student at the Royal Academy Schools during the last decade of the eighteenth century. Many of his watercolours during this period are topographical studies both in technique and subject matter. Turner made many sketching tours throughout Britain and he chose a wide range of subjects which included cathedrals, castles, country estates and scenic views, particularly mountain ones. By the mid 1790s he became familiar with seventeenth and eighteenth-century engravings of Italian landscape views. These pictures were painted in a classical manner by artists such as Claude Lorrain and Richard Wilson, both artists Turner greatly admired. He showed his first oil painting at the Academy while still a pupil there in 1796. In 1802 travel to Europe again became possible and Turner made his first visit to the Alps, where he recorded the mountain scenery in watercolour. Turner may well have used the knowledge he first acquired in the mountains of Snowdonia in 1798 and 1799. From 1840, following adverse criticism of his oil paintings, his work was defended and championed by the art critic and patron John Ruskin (1819–1900).

Ruskin's support continued for the rest of Turner's career, and it was Ruskin who catalogued the majority of works left to the nation in the Turner bequest.

This large coloured drawing was made outside in the open air. On this tour to north Wales Turner brought along a set of large drawing sheets that were temporarily folded, in addition to his usual sketchbooks. This is one of these large sheets. Turner would have come to this comparatively remote area of Snowdonia to see for himself the view that Richard Wilson had originally painted in the mid 1760s and later issued as an engraved print. It is very likely that Turner was also following the suggested route as described by Thomas Pennant in *The Journey to Snowdon* section of his book. The Wilson painting shows a distant view of Snowdon and Turner has moved further up the valley, above the lakes, to get a closer view towards the mountain. The foreground area of the sketch is unfinished, suggesting he was in a hurry. There is another much slighter sketch showing the Nantlle lakes with Snowdon beyond made on the same visit.

16. J. M. W. Turner, Y Garn with Snowdon in the Distance, from above Llyn Nantlle, *1799. gouache, graphite and watercolour on paper, 55.7 x 76.8. Tate Britain*

17
Thomas Mann Baynes, *Snowdon from Nantlle*, c.1825, lithograph, 10.2 x 15.3, in Rev. G. J. Freeman, *Sketches in Wales; or a Diary of Three Walking Excursions in that Principality, in the years 1823, 1824, 1825*, London, 1826, plate 13

Thomas Mann Baynes (1794–1854) was the artist commissioned to make the illustrations for the Reverend G. J. Freeman's travel book published in 1826. This was a record of three walking tours to north Wales made in the 1820s, at a time when walking tours had become fashionable. Freeman visited the Nantlle lakes during his third excursion to north Wales in 1825. He acknowledged Wilson's prior visual claim to the site when he wrote, 'Wilson took his celebrated and most accurate view of Snowdon. No scene is finer that I know...'[4] Freeman inserted fifteen lithographs to illustrate his text. Thomas Mann Baynes was both a watercolour artist and a lithographer. Monochrome lithography was a relatively new process and was ideally suited for the reproduction of tonal areas associated with watercolour.

Snowdon from Nantlle by Baynes shows a view taken from a point further up the vale, on the left and closer to the top of the first lake than in Wilson's view. In Baynes' print there is no foreground from which to enter this landscape. The picture is set high and the viewer is suspended above an invisible foreground. This produces a feeling of disquiet in an otherwise placid scene. The composition is dominated by the jagged profiles of the enclosing Drws-y-Coed on the right and the more threatening shape of Mynydd Mawr on the left. Through the gap in the middle Snowdon rises in a softer tone skywards. At the top of Snowdon a cloud obscures part of the summit peak, a pictorial device that Wilson had also applied to his view of Snowdon.

Views of Snowdon 57

17. Thomas Mann Baynes, Snowdon from Nantlle, *c.1825, lithograph, 10.2 x 15.3, in Rev. G J Freeman,* Sketches in Wales, *London, 1826, plate 13*

18
Joshua Cristall, *Aber Llan from Plas Gwynant,* **c.1820, pen over traces of pencil on paper, 25.4 x 35.8, private collection**

Joshua Cristall (1767–1847) was born in Camborne in Cornwall but grew up in London. Originally apprenticed as a painter of porcelain in Shropshire, he abandoned this and returned to London in 1792. He became a student at the Royal Academy schools where he came to the attention of Dr Thomas Munro (1759–1833) and met the the group of young artists associated with Munro's 'circle' which included J. M. W. Turner. By 1802 Cristall was an accomplished artist and he made his first tour to north Wales, meeting up with John and Cornelius Varley and William Havell at Dolgellau. The following year he returned to north Wales with Cornelius Varley. Further visits were made in 1820 and in 1831. Cristall exhibited a watercolour at the first exhibition of the Old Watercolour Society in 1805 and also showed at the Royal Academy. Although he is known to have visited Scotland and the Lake District several times, it was his Welsh experience that most influenced his pastoral works, and it was Welsh subjects that dominated his exhibits at the Watercolour Society. Apart from his landscape watercolours, Cristall had a facility for figure painting and many of these studies are exquisite. He moved to Goodrich in 1822 and concentrated on painting the local farm labourers of the locality. Thomas Tudor was a neighbour and friend. Following his wife's death Cristall returned to London in 1841. He continued working until his death in 1847 and is buried alongside his wife in Goodrich, Herefordshire.

In *Aber Llan from Plas Gynant* Cristall has chosen an elevated viewpoint looking across Cwm Llan towards the heights of Snowdon. This line drawing has been carefully composed so the image fills the whole sheet of paper. The use of line gives solidity to the whole picture. This gives the drawing a decorative aspect which combines with an accurate portrayal of the topographical features of the location. The trees are almost abstract in their forms but retain a strong visual identity that complements the profile of Snowdon at the top of the drawing. The lack of sky emphasises the height of Snowdon and its associated mountain landscape. The linear treatment and the creation of abstract areas between the drawn lines feels very modern in its depiction of visual space.

18. Joshua Cristall, Aber Llan from Plas Gwynant, *c.1820, pen over traces of pencil on paper, 25.4 x 35.8, private collection*

19
Sidney Richard Percy, *In Snowdonia*, 1853, oil on canvas, 55.2 x 78.9, Tate Britain

Sidney Richard Percy (1821–1886) was a London-based landscape painter in oil. He was born into the Williams family of artists and, after 1841, he replaced Williams with Percy to differentiate him from the other artists in the family. He received his art tuition from his father Edward Williams (1781–1855), a successful landscape artist. He showed at the Royal Academy from 1842 onwards and exhibited at the British Institution and at the Society of British Artists in Suffolk Street. He lived in Barnes from 1846 and shared a studio with other members of the Williams family. In 1857 he was living in Wandsworth, and later lived at Great Missenden with easy access to a variety of landscape subjects. As a landscape painter he visited north Wales and the Lake District in search of mountain scenery. He also went to the north of England and Scotland. He travelled abroad in 1865, visiting Italy, Switzerland and France. The conflict between Prussia and Austria curtailed a return visit and he ventured back to north Wales and worked in the area around Llanbedr and the Mawddach estuary and Cader Idris. During these visits S. R. Percy made small, on-the-spot studies in watercolour and these were later used as information for the finished realist oil paintings. In his later years he lived at Sutton in Surrey. His untimely death in 1886 was caused by complications after his leg was amputated following a horse-riding accident.

In Snowdonia depicts a close-up view of Snowdon with a cloud-free summit. This view is taken from the east side of the mountain. The composition is carefully constructed with the peak of Snowdon set on the golden section. This leads the eye to the summit which is the focal point of the painting. The realism of this picture is achieved by the use of a sharp focused technique applied evenly to the whole picture surface. S. R. Percy had an interest in photography and had used his own photographic figure studies for the foregrounds of a number of landscape paintings. The level of realism we see in this painting was beyond anything photography could produce during this period, particularly in colour. In the painting the colour is very carefully applied, using a limited range of hues with enough differentiation to keep the painting alive and fresh in spite of such a restricted palette of earthy browns and rocky greys. All this is contrasted against the clear light blue sky, with its pinkish clouds heading towards the summit and acting as a counterbalance to the pyramid shape of Snowdon itself.

19. Sidney Richard Percy, In Snowdonia, *1853, oil on canvas, 55.2 x 78.9, Tate Britain*

20
Henry Clarence Whaite, *The Heart of Snowdon*, c.1907, oil on canvas, 142.2 x 173.3, National Museums Liverpool

Henry Clarence Whaite (1828–1912) was a landscape painter who trained at the Manchester School of Design and then attended classes at the Royal Academy Schools in London. A visit to Switzerland around 1850 introduced him to mountain scenery. In 1851 he visited north Wales and explored the area's potential for mountain subjects. Later, he moved to live near Betws-y-coed, where he became a leading figure in the artistic community. His mountain paintings of Snowdonia are meticulously observed. However the forms are often dissolving out of focus, as, like David Cox, he was a painter of the weather conditions encountered in the mountains. Whaite showed at the Royal Academy from 1859 and was noticed there by John Ruskin. His style of painting and the sense of the epic has a strong affinity with the work of the American painter of mountains, Frederick Edwin Church (1826–1900). Church exhibited his large oil painting, *The Heart of the Andes* (1859) in London in the Summer of 1859 and it is likely that Whaite saw it exhibited there. The artist may have borrowed the title for his own later painting, substituting 'Snowdon' for 'Andes' in the title. The large scale, attention to minute detail, close observation of nature along Ruskinian lines, and mountain subject matter of Church's painting would have been inspirational for Whaite. He helped to set up the Manchester Academy of Fine Art in 1859 and later the original Cambrian Academy. He continued to live in the Conwy valley until his death in 1907.

The Heart of Snowdon shows a close-up view of the mountain through a moody mist, which pervades the sublime scene. Whaite often made composite landscape views where various activities or landscape features are recomposed into a new image. This painting is probably a composite view but it conveys the essence of the experience of Welsh mountain scenery and its changeable weather. The deep grey blue of Snowdon is the complementary colour to the orange browns of the foreground rocks that frame the view. This painting is in the possession of the Walker Art Gallery, Liverpool.

20. Henry Clarence Whaite, The Heart of Snowdon, *c.1907, oil on canvas, 142.2 x 173.3, National Museums Liverpool*

21
Kyffin Williams, *Snowdon from Drws y Coed*, c.1965, oil on canvas, 119.8 x 181.6, Bangor University

Kyffin Williams (1918-2006) was educated at Shrewsbury School, a marked contrast to his country childhood in Llangefni on Anglesey. He was discharged from the army in 1941 for health reasons, as he suffered from epilepsy, and was advised to study art. He attended the Slade School of Fine Art, then in its temporary home in Oxford, from 1941 to 1944. After the Slade, he secured a part-time teaching post at Highgate School in north London, which he held from 1944 to 1973. Returning to Anglesey, he lived in a cottage on the edge of the Menai Strait with a panoramic view towards Snowdon. Kyffin Williams was elected a full member of the Royal Academy in 1974. He was elected President of the Royal Cambrian Academy twice, and did much to revitalise the fortunes of the Academy in Conwy with the establishment of a new gallery. There are over 325 paintings by Kyffin Williams in public collections.

Snowdon from Drws y Coed depicts the triangular summit peak of Snowdon as seen from Drws-y-Coed. The summit peak is the main focus of the painting's composition, and it is framed by steep mountain slopes on both sides of the foreground area. The artist has used a tripartite compositional formula of side screens and background as promoted by William Gilpin in his many picturesque guides. However, Kyffin Williams' picture is not 'picturesque' in the Gilpin sense: it is a fairly harsh rendering of the view. The roughness of the impasto technique along with the strong tonal contrast add to the feeling of desolation as encountered in the higher regions of Snowdonia. A characteristic of many of Kyffin Williams' mountain paintings is the restricted colour he applies to his paintings. In this example he uses strong dark grey-black colour for Snowdon and the tops of the framing rocks on either side. These dark areas form a compositional crescent, below which the warmer ochres and yellow-browns of the foreground lead the eye into the painting. Kyffin Williams preferred to paint the changeable weather conditions in his mountain landscapes as these added drama and elements of the sublime to his paintings.

21. Kyffin Williams, *Snowdon from Drws y Coed, c.1965, oil on canvas, 119.8 x 181.6, Bangor University*

22
David Tress, *Light Passing (Llyn Llydaw) Towards Snowdon*, 2007, mixed media on paper, 57 x 77, Tabernacl collection, Museum of Modern Art Wales, Machynlleth, Powys.

David Tress (b.1955) grew up in London and was a student at Harrow College of Art before studying fine art at Nottingham Trent University, from where he graduated in 1976. The same year he moved to Pembrokeshire so he could devote his time to working as a professional artist. He is primarily a landscape painter and has worked in Continental Europe and the United States as well as Scotland, the Lake District and Wales. Tress has also made city landscapes particularly of London over a number of years. In1992 he was elected to the Royal Cambrian Academy based in Conwy, north Wales. He has also served on the Welsh Arts Council and, in 1999, was commissioned to produce a stamp as part of a set of stamps by various artists to celebrate the Millennium, published by the Royal Mail in 2000. In 2013 David Tress was awarded the Glyndwr Award for an outstanding contribution to the arts in Wales.

From the mid eighties onwards his painting style became more evocative, combining elements of gestural abstraction with an emotional expressionism that is very much his own. These mixed media works, often made on heavy paper, comprise a range of approaches including scraping and adding layers of paper - each part contributing to the finished whole. His mixed media monochrome drawings are strong tonal works and the retention of areas of white paper produce powerful evocations of the landscape. David Tress has exhibited widely throughout Britain and his work is in many private and public collections including: National Museums of Wales, National Library of Wales, MOMA Wales, Pallant House, Chichester and the Guild Hall, City of London. David Tress is represented by Messum's, London.

In *Light Passing (Llyn Llydaw) Towards Snowdon* the artist has portrayed the sombre gloom of the location as witnessed at first hand. The picturesque is not much in evidence here, rather a sublime feeling of foreboding is present. A type of light that only seems to be present in the Snowdon area is depicted and this ethereal quality of light is referred to by the artist in the title he gave to the work. The composition adheres to the golden mean with the lighter part of sky at top left and the blue grey of the lake making another divide in the composition. The whole image is enlivened by small patches of orange and red colour. The technique Tress has used in this work mirrors the same conditions he encountered at the time. The heavily encrusted paper layering in the middle left section along with thin streaks of coloured paint all reflect the transient nature of both his working methods and the reality of the subject. This can be seen in the use of strong dark tones with the surface retaining an energy that pervades the whole area of the picture. This work was made in the studio from drawings and notes made on location.

22. *David Tress,* Light Passing (Llyn Llydaw) Towards Snowdon, *2007, mixed media on paper, 57 x 77, MOMA, Wales*

23
Robert A Newell, *Clogwyn Du'r Arddu,* 2012, oil on canvas, 106.7 x 152.5, collection of the artist

Robert Newell (born 1952) is a landscape painter who specialises in the geological aspect of landscape, particularly in the rhythms associated with rock strata. He studied Fine Art at Wimbledon School of Art from 1973–1977, gaining a BA, and later at Goldsmiths College, University of London from 1982–1984, where he was awarded an MA. He obtained a PhD from the University of Wales in 2005. In 1993 he became a senior lecturer in Visual Studies at Swansea Institute of Higher Education, which became Swansea Metropolitan University. Since 1996 he has worked as a fractional Associate Lecturer in Fine Art at what is now Swansea Metropolitan, University of Wales Trinity Saint David. The main focus of his recent research and painting has been connected with the coastal regions and the mountains of Wales. His drawings are carefully observed analytical studies made on location. These are often used as a starting point for the larger intensely observed paintings. These works embody concerns of the 'truth to nature' dictum that Ruskin had made explicit in *Modern Painters*, published between 1843–1860. Newell has been a member of the Royal Cambrian Academy since 2002. He has exhibited widely in both group and solo exhibitions. His work is represented in both private and public collections throughout the UK.

In *Clogwyn Du'r Arddu* we are presented with a powerful emblematic image of the north flank of Snowdon. Newell has used minutely observed detail to capture every fissure and rock type visible, in a light that is particular to the higher Welsh peaks, uniting the rocks with the sky. The painting's main focus is on the rugged terrain of the near-vertical cliffs and this is further emphasised by the lack of sky in the composition. The artist has stated that rocks are a source of fascination for him and that he is absorbed by the way varying conditions of light and atmosphere contribute to the aesthetic power of landscape. Newell's picture of Clogwyn Du'r Arddu adheres to the artist's principal aims in landscape painting and is a fine example of his work.

23. Robert Newell, Clogwyn Du'r Arddu, 2012, oil on canvas, 106.7 x 152.5, collection of the artist

FOUR
Sketching on the Move

The heyday for making a tour to Snowdonia was the first quarter of the nineteenth century, although the fashion for making a 'picturesque' tour had already become well established by this time. The idea of making a picturesque tour of north Wales attracted tourists as well as artists. Some visitors were clergymen who had a long summer break and could afford both the time and the cost of making a visit. Others were well-to-do Gentlemen who could afford to stay in the new hotels that had recently been constructed to meet the increasing demand for overnight accommodation.

A visit to the rugged mountain scenery of Snowdonia required careful preparation. Advice was available in a large number of the published guide books, obtainable from book shops that also sold prints and maps such as John Evan's fold-out map of north Wales, first published in 1795. The advice offered in the travel literature included which route to follow and where the best views of mountain scenery could be found. Other advice included what clothing was most appropriate, and even what size sketchbook to take and which drawing materials to use. The books even recommended which local guides to hire for an ascent of a mountain such as Cader Idris. The ascent of Cader Idris was usually made from the Royal Ship Hotel in Dolgellau, often accompanied by a hired guide.

Many of these recently published guides were fairly slim volumes and contained an itinerary, and often a map of the tour route. They were portable and often illustrated with views by the author or commissioned from a professional artist. These were engraved as plates and placed adjacent to the written passage that described the location.

Artists making a tour to north Wales to collect material for their work were often restricted by the inclement weather and the need to work quickly, particularly if they were part of a touring party with an accommodation deadline to meet. The favoured time to visit was early summer. June was a popular month. High summer was avoided if possible because of hazy conditions. September was another month when conditions became favourable.

Travelling through this rough terrain required either horses or hired Welsh ponies, although pedestrian tours were a way of exploring the country. A combination of both methods of travel proved popular. Sketching on the move is as popular today as it was when Paul Sandby (1731–1809) visited Snowdonia in the early 1770s.

Freeman on the mode of travel on a tour:

A man may be well excused, if he hurries over a district which he sufficiently knows, or whose features are disagreeable. But the only way he has to make himself well acquainted with a country, is by passing through it leisurely, and on foot.

G K Freeman, Sketches in Wales, London, 1826, p.vii.

Detail of Plate 24. Paul Sandby. View of the River Dee 3 Miles Short of Bala.

Plates 24-30

24
Paul Sandby. ***View of the River Dee 3 Miles Short of Bala, with Cader Idris Mountain near Dolgelli 30 Miles Distant*, 1777, aquatint print, 23.7 x 31.4, drawn and published by Paul Sandby, London, private collection**

Paul Sandby (1731–1809) was a topographical watercolour artist and publisher of the first aquatints in Britain; a process which he helped to develop. Sandby made the first recorded tour to north Wales in 1771. This tour lasted two weeks and the large touring party consisted of Sir Watkin Williams Wynn (1749–1789), his guests, the artist Sandby and nine servants and horses. Sandby was engaged as a drawing master and to record the scenery encountered on the tour in both pencil and watercolour. The party left Wynnstay on 21st August, returning there on 4th September. Some of the views Sandby sketched on this visit were reproduced as aquatint prints in his sets of views in Wales. The first set of prints had featured views in south Wales. These sets of prints were advertised in Thomas Pennant's *A Tour in Wales* and helped to promote the landscape of north Wales. Sandby's aquatint prints inspired many travellers, tourists and artists to make a picturesque tour to north Wales. This was fast becoming a fashionable activity and sketching on the move heralded the arrival of the Romantic Movement.

Sandby's aquatint print, *View of the River Dee 3 Miles short of Bala ...* is plate nine from *XII Views in South and North Wales*, published in 1777. Sandby arrived at this location around 23rd August at the start of the 1771 tour. The picture shows Sir Watkin Williams Wynn's touring party on route to Bala with Cader Idris in the far distance. Sandby has depicted himself on a rock, silhouetted against the light while sketching the mountain scenery in front of him. This aspect of a transient moment is reflected in the long descriptive title that Sandby gave to this print with its emphasis on travelling. The aquatint process originally came to England from France and Sandby exploited its full potential to reproduce the tonal values of watercolour. The colour used to print the image, as in this example, is a rich sepia brown that allows a large range of tonal values to be present but is not as harsh as the monochrome inks used in more conventional prints of the period. This image conveys the excitement of travelling through a mountainous area and sketching on the move.

24. *Paul Sandby.* View of the River Dee 3 Miles Short of Bala, *1777, aquatint print, 23.7 x 31.4, drawn and published by Paul Sandby, London, private collection*

25
Cornelius Varley, *Panorama of Cader Idris from Llanelltyd, NW*, 1803, pencil and grey wash on paper, 26.7 x 43.5, Courtauld Institute of Art, London

Cornelius Varley (1781–1873) was a draughtsman and watercolour artist. His early education was in the natural sciences and instrument-making. From about 1800 he began to study art and went on a tour to north Wales in 1802 with his brother John Varley (1778–1842), also an artist. He returned there the following year with the artist Joshua Cristall (1767–1847). He made further sketching tours to north Wales with other artists and exhibited at the Royal Academy and at the Watercolour Society exhibitions. Cornelius Varley invented the graphic telescope, which was patented in 1811. This was an optical instrument that enabled artists to project a magnified image onto a sheet of paper. It was particularly helpful for making accurate portrait drawings. He also had an interest in astronomy and from 1845 he recorded comets and stars seen through his improved graphic telescope. His landscape drawings and watercolours, particularly those made in Wales, did not follow the picturesque conventions of the day; rather, they were more accurate transcriptions of place, no doubt influenced by the use of the graphic telescope, which he sometimes employed in his landscape drawings.

Cornelius Varley drew *Cader Idris from Llanelltyd NW* while on his second tour to north Wales in 1803. Llanelltyd is a small village two miles north of Dolgellau with the river Wnion between. The drawing shows a panorama of the the mountain seen from a vantage point above the village. In this expansive drawing the mountain profile is carefully drawn, with the broad sweep of the valley highlighted by deft touches of grey watercolour washes. This combination of drawn pencil line and grey wash gives a vitality to the whole drawing. In the middle distance, at left, the bridge over the river is depicted using the minimum of marks yet conveying the actuality of the structure. Varley made another sketch of this vista towards Cader Idris from this location on the same visit, titled, *Mountain Panorama in Wales – Cader Idris* which is in the Yale Centre for British Art. It is the same size and is likely to be from the same or a similar sketchbook. This drawing is less finished but the weather conditions have been recorded by Varley at the bottom of the drawing. The inscription reads, 'Fine weather wind S.E. Clouds coming towards me ... but dissolved into transparent atmosphere as fast as they came so that I had constant blue sky overhead'. There are two other short notes referring to the sun. Another Varley sketchbook is in the collection of the Morgan Library and Museum, New York. It contains two panoramic drawings dated 1803 of this view on joined sheets of paper in a mix of drawing media. It might be suggested that this view of Cader Idris was a particular favourite of the artist.

25. Cornelius Varley, *Panorama of Cader Idris from Llanelltyd NW*, 1803, pencil and grey wash on paper, 26.7 x 43.5, Courtauld Institute of Art, London

26
Sir John James Stewart, *Cader Idris from the road between Barmouth and Dolgelly NW*, c.1820, watercolour over traces of pencil, 10.5 x 15, private collection

Sir John James Stewart (1779–1849) was primarily known for his military drawings and battle scenes usually in watercolour. A series of military and equestrian subjects were published as etchings in 1821. A collection of these prints is in the Harvard Art Museum in Cambridge, Massachusetts. He also made tinted watercolour drawings of places and probably visited north Wales around 1820.

Cader Idris from the road between Barmouth and Dolgelly is likely to date from 1820. This view is drawn in pencil with watercolour washes applied directly to provide a visual memoranda of the scene made while travelling. The location is highlighted by the title inscribed underneath the picture area. This watercolour is a transcription of place made simply from direct observation in just a few minutes. Sir John James Stewart was primarily a military artist, yet such was the popularity of the north Wales tour at this time that it attracted a wide range of artists, not all of whom were landscape painters. The road along the Mawddach estuary between Dolgellau and Barmouth presents a fine profile of Cader Idris, seen to the south. This location is one of the most beautiful in the whole of Wales.

The pedestrian tour and speed of travel:

Three miles an hour would be found fast enough for tour pursuit: and twelve to fourteen miles a day for two months would carry you through a considerable tour, allowing for a halt on the march, sometimes for two or three days, in order to explore. Your principal object is to exercise your pencil...

R H Newell, Letters on the Scenery of Wales, 1821, p.3.

Advice on footwear and clothing from Newell in the early 1820s:

Shoes, stout, broad, well seasoned, made for each foot and without nails - they are dangerous on rocky ground. Top the whole with a straw or rather a willow hat. Nor must an umbrella by any means be forgotten, it is a truly useful servant, choose it of silk and of the largest size.

R H Newell, Letters on the Scenery of Wales, 1821, p.9.

26. *Sir John James Stewart (attributed)*, Cader Idris from the road between Barmouth and Dolgelly *NW, c. 1820, watercolour over traces of pencil, 10.5 x 15, private collection*

27
Thomas Tudor of Monmouth, *Near Dolgelly*, c.1820, pencil and pen on paper, 13 x 22.5, private collection

Thomas Tudor (1785–1855) was a semi-professional artist and art collector who lived in Monmouth. A friend of the artist Joshua Cristall, a successful watercolour artist, Tudor combined a career as a land agent with making watercolours of landscape, especially of the picturesque river Wye. Interestingly, many of these works are unfinished. He made several excursions to north Wales from his home in Monmouthshire.

Near Dolgelly as inscribed by Tudor depicts a view towards Cader Idris from a viewpoint close to the village of Llanelltyd, 2 miles north of Dolgellau. The viewpoint for this line drawing is from a bend in the river below the village. The arches of the bridge have been drawn with a simplicity of form. It was quite common for artists to overlay pen on top of their pencil outlines at a later date. The paper for this drawing is watermarked 1817 and suggests a probable date of 1820 or 1832 for this sketch, as Tudor is known to have visited north Wales in both of these years. The drawing shows the bridge over the Wnion with the profile of Cader Idris in the background filling the rest of the picture.

27. Thomas Tudor of Monmouth, Near Dolgelly, c. 1820, pencil and pen on paper, 13 x 22.5, private collection

28
Joshua Cristall, *The summit of Cader Idris, Dolgelly side*, 1820, pencil on paper, 20 x 34, private collection

Joshua Cristall (1767–1847) was a watercolour painter who studied at the Royal Academy Schools in London and became part of the circle of artists who attended the 'Academy' of Dr Thomas Munro. Here he met J. M. W. Turner and Thomas Girtin. He travelled extensively throughout Britain and made several tours to north Wales between 1802 and 1832.

The summit of Cader Idris, Dolgelly side was drawn on location on Cristall's 1820 tour to north Wales. It was a view Cristall was familiar with from his previous visits to the area. It depicts the vista towards the main summits of the mountain seen across the vale from close to the village of Llanelltyd, a few miles north of Dolgellau. From this elevated viewpoint an attractive panorama of Cader Idris comes into view. Cristall has made a line drawing that adheres to the landscape structure and compositional integrity of the actual view and is a fully worked up drawing made on the spot.

> On sketchbook sizes:
>
> *The sketchbooks I have used are two, about nine inches long by six and three-quarters wide, containing thirty leaves each, and three smaller about four inches and a half long by six and three-quarters wide. All of these should be made of thin hot pressed paper, this takes the pencil best, is most portable.*
>
> R H Newell, *Letters on the Scenery of Wales*, 1821, p.15.

28. *Joshua Cristall,* The summit of Cader Idris, Dolgelly side, *1820, pencil on paper, 20 x 34, private collection*

29
Kevan Hopson, *Cader Idris from near Llanelltyd,* **2013, mixed media drawing on paper, 25 x 27, private collection**

Kevan Hopson (b.1958) is a professional artist who produces work in both 2D and 3D media. He is a graduate of Bedford College, University of London, where he gained an honours degree in mathematics in 1983. After teaching in his home county of Hertfordshire he embarked on his art career and moved to mid Wales in 1985. His sculptures are mainly carved from driftwood collected from the beaches of mid Wales. The finished forms of his sculptures owe much to the suggested form of the original piece with any intervention sympathetically applied. These pieces often emerge from his studio as ornithological subjects. Hopson also works in watercolour and these are focused on the varied mountain scenery of Snowdonia and the landscape close to his studio near Welshpool. In 1998 he was selected to represent Wales at the Welsh Fair in Brussels. His work is collected nationally and internationally and since 1995 he has been represented by Cambridge Contemporary Art. His work is in both private and public collections in the UK and abroad.

Cader Idris from near Llanelltyd has been made on location using a variety of combined media to record the artist's immediate response to the subject seen. In this sketchbook drawing Hopson has used water-soluble pencil, chalk-pastel and watercolour to capture the essence of the view towards Cader Idris. The image, apart from recording the scene, is imaginatively improvised further by the artist to allow for a personal response to the view that is much more than a topographical record of place. The overall loose painterly technique and restricted colour gives immediacy to the picture. The composition is presented as emblematic with its lack of recessional space emphasising the mountain's height. The sky acts as a counterbalance to the mountain forms and is integral to the picture's overall appearance. Hopson makes a number of sketches at one location while travelling through the mountains of Wales and many embody an imaginative element as well. Some of these sketches become the starting point for larger works painted in his mid Wales studio.

29. *Kevan Hopson,* Cader Idris from near Llanellytd, *2013, mixed media drawing on paper, 25 x 27, private collection*

30
Matthew Wood, *Snowdonia from Nebo*, 2013, oil on board, 9 x 21, private collection

Matthew Wood (b.1973) is a painter specialising in Welsh landscape. After a Foundation course at Shrewsbury School of Art he studied painting at Middlesex University London, graduating with a BA honours degree in Fine Art in 1998. Wood obtained a PGCE from the Birmingham Institute of Art and Design in 1999. From 2000 to 2001 he studied on a post-graduate course in painting at the School of Art, Aberystwyth University, where he was awarded an MA in Fine Art. After completing his MA, Wood made the decision to move to mid Wales to concentrate on painting the Welsh landscape. His oil paintings are made solely on location and are executed in one sitting on fabricated panels, a method of painting that recalls Georges Seurat (1859–1891) and his use of cigar box lids for his plein air oil studies. In Wood's pictures of Welsh mountain scenery the oil paint is applied directly and embraces the climatic conditions as they are at the time of working. The subjects range from landscapes close to his studio to the high mountains of Snowdonia. He has exhibited widely, and in 2008 had a painting of an interior exhibited at the prestigious John Moores 25 exhibition at the Walker Art Gallery, Liverpool.

Snowdonia from Nebo was painted in oils directly from nature at a viewpoint above the Conwy valley, to the east of Betws-y-coed. The view seen here presents a panorama of Snowdonia's highest mountains. In this plein air painting the artist has depicted the Glyders on the left, Tryfan in the middle distance, the Ogwen valley, and to the right is Carnedd

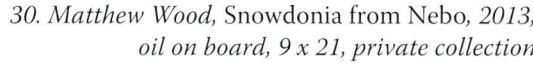

30. Matthew Wood, Snowdonia from Nebo, *2013, oil on board, 9 x 21, private collection*

Dafydd. The view caught the artist's eye whilst taking a back route to Llanrwst from the A5. At the time, in late June, Wood recorded in a note that, 'the greens were translating into some stunning tones of greys and blues in the middle distance'. There is an immediacy in Wood's small paintings that include the weather conditions encountered at the time on the uplands of Snowdonia and this slightly rough quality is often a feature of these paintings made outside in the landscape. The alla-prima technique the artist employs, and the carefully judged colour, give a vision of mountain scenery that Wood has made his own.

FIVE
Views of Cader Idris

Cader Idris (893 m) is a mountain situated between Dolgellau and the sea, in the south of Snowdonia. In the mid 1760s Richard Wilson (1713–1782) painted a view from Mynydd Moel (863 m) on the shoulder of Cadair Idris looking towards a lake with a mountain backdrop. This painting, *Llyn-y-Cau, Cader Idris* can be seen as complementary to the view of Snowdon (discussed in chapter Three). Both pictures show a lake with a mountain backdrop, but in the Cader Idris painting the vista is restricted by the imposing bulk of the cliff faces rising above Llyn y Cau. This picture was engraved and published in 1775 by John Boydell. It was the sixth print in the set.

As with Wilson's *Snowdon*, the published prints, along with Paul Sandby's aquatints of mountain scenery, did much to enhance the attraction of Cader Idris as a mountain that could be visited while on a picturesque tour. An ascent of Cader Idris could be made by pony from Dolgellau, a distance of about five miles. Some visitors hired guides to accompany them on their visit to the heights of Cadair Idris. When J M W Turner came here on his 1798 tour in search of Wilson's viewpoint, he was a victim of dreadfully wet conditions that obliterated the mountain scenery from view. In Turner's sketchbook made on Cader Idris there are watercolours distorted with large rain drops. By 1800 Cader Idris was being visited by tourists and artists in ever increasing numbers during the summer months. The relative accessibility of Cader Idris; the improved hotel accommodation in Dolgellau; its varied scenery; all were contributory factors that met the requirements of visitors and artists in search of dramatic mountain scenery.

A visit to Cader Idris was usually made in small groups sometimes accompanied by a guide. A small group of artists made a tour in 1803 and visited Cader Idris; they were, Cornelius Varley, (1781–1873), his brother, John Varley (1778–1848), Joshua Cristall (1767–1847) and William Havell (1782–1857). They made an ascent of the mountain that included a visit to the actual viewpoint chosen by Wilson for his picture. A watercolour drawn on the spot by Cornelius Varley is inscribed 'Wilson's Pool', acknowledging Wilson's prior association with the view. As the nineteenth century progressed the mountain and its many and varied viewpoints, distant, close up, high or low, and of Llyn-y-Cau in particular, became increasingly favoured by visiting artists such as David Cox (1783 –1859).

By the second half of the nineteenth century references to Wilson's painting were absent from the guidebooks such as *Black's Picturesque Guide to North Wales*, published from 1851 onwards, either in written or pictorial form. The twentieth century was a period when many artists were focused on other subjects, but artists such as Kyffin Williams (1918-2006) re-examined the mountain and made several oil paintings including views of Llyn-y-Cau from Wilson's high vantage point on Mynydd Moel.

The attraction of Cader Idris for artists has continued into the twenty-first century. Today only a few people venture to Wilson's viewpoint close to Mynydd Moel. Among those who have is Pete Davis (b.1947) who has made large monochrome photographs documenting the mountain from various places and in a wide range of weather conditions. In 2001 an exhibition 'Cader Idris' was held, in which some sixty twentieth and twenty-first century works were exhibited.[5] Although the mountain occupies a relatively small geographic area, it is capable of yielding an almost infinite range of visual stimuli, and clearly still holds a fascination for artists who wish to capture that sense of awe in front of untamed nature.

Detail of Plate 31. Richard Wilson, Llyn-y-Cau, Cader Idris

Plates 31-39

31
Richard Wilson, *Llyn-y-Cau, Cader Idris*, c.1765-7, oil on canvas, 50 x 72, Tate Britain, London

Richard Wilson (1713–1782) painted his Welsh landscapes after his return from Italy in 1757. In Italy he had met Francesco Zuccarelli (1702–1788), who introduced him to landscape painting, and Wilson painted his portrait in Venice in 1751. Wilson also came into contact with the works of Claude Lorrain (c.1604–1682) and many other Italianate classical landscape artists of the period. Their classical compositions greatly influenced his landscape painting. While in Rome he visited the locations selected by Claude for his views of the Italian campagna, originally painted in the seventeenth century. Classical landscape paintings were collected by the landed gentry in Britain who filled their country houses with them and modelled their landscaped gardens to look like the paintings of the campagna. Wilson's commissioned paintings took account of this connection between the remodelled landscape acres outside and the painted classical landscapes hanging on the walls inside. This connection was aptly summed up when the poet William Cowper (1731–1800) wrote in 'The Task', published in 1785:

I admire – None more admires – the painter's magic skill
Who shows me that which I shall never see,
Conveys a distant country into mine,
And throws Italian light on English walls.

In *Llyn-y-Cau, Cader Idris* we are presented with a rugged mountain landscape vista observed from the slopes of Mynydd Moel. Wilson depicts a contemporary landscape full of human activity. The figures, as in the Snowdon painting, are disguised by the classical treatment that Wilson has applied throughout the painting. This treatment allows one of the most desolate and potentially dangerous locations in north Wales to be immediately accessible and non-threatening.

The viewpoint, as in the Snowdon painting, is just left of centre but now it is taken from an elevated position. In *Llyn-y-Cau, Cader Idris* there is little foreground interruption and the viewer can see the deep space of the Dysynni Valley on the extreme left. Alternatively, the eye is led straight ahead to contemplate the lake and beyond this the summit ridge of Mynydd Pen coed, a part of Cader Idris, is on the far right. The summit itself is beyond the picture frame. Wilson has presented a mountain landscape that is under the control and ownership of man. A party of visitors have made an ascent and are shown engaged in various activities. In the near foreground is a figure scanning the southern horizon with a telescope. This gentleman is using the latest portable optical device recently developed in London. His long shadow indicates that an early morning ascent has been made. He is a member of the touring party who are now scattered across the mountain. On the opposite side is a seated figure, possibly Wilson himself, sketching the view towards the rocky summit itself. Two other figures are shown in sunlight above the lake contemplating the scenery. Beyond them, to the right, two further figures are by the lakeshore. There is a figure present who is not a member of the touring party, standing next to a grazing animal. The use of high summer grazing on the Welsh mountains was a common sight in the eighteenth century but is rarely seen today

31. Richard Wilson, Llyn-y-Cau, Cader Idris, *c.1765-7, oil on canvas, 50 x 72, Tate Britain, London*

32
Thomas Tudor, *Cader Idris*, 1802, pencil and wash on paper, 28.5 x 27.5, National Library of Wales, Aberystwyth

Thomas Tudor (1785–1855) lived in Monmouth where he was a land agent. His father Owen, ran a successful book shop in the centre of Monmouth. Here Thomas would have come into contact with the topographical engravings to be seen in the shop. At the age of thirteen or so he and his brother, John, contributed illustrations for William Coxe, *An Historical Tour in Monmouthshire*, published in 1801. Through the book-selling business Thomas came into contact with a range of visitors, and his father encouraged his artistic talent. He made a number of sketching tours to north Wales between 1802 and 1832. Tudor exhibited at the Royal Academy, London, from 1809 to 1819. He formed his own art collection, which included a work by J. M. W. Turner. Although Tudor painted a number of works in oil, it is his watercolours that are most accomplished.

Thomas Tudor made this monochrome wash drawing of Cader Idris in 1802 while on the first of his many tours of north Wales. He came to Cader Idris again in 1820. Tudor was a keen traveller and made other tours in Wales; the picturesque river Wye was a favourite subject.

Tudor's watercolour of Cader Idris has been made quickly on the spot. Its emblematic quality perfectly captures the spirit of place. The absence of detail and colour in this picture reinforces the monumental aspect of the location. This is all achieved by the use of Gilpin's compositional formula of side screens but on this occasion it is the sublime that pervades the picture not the picturesque.

An ascent of Cader Idris by Joseph Craddock:

... here I must acknowledge my head was too giddy sufficiently to admire the amazing scene that was opening to my view. At length, ... I could with comfort survey the sea, the Caernarvonshire shore, Snowdon without a cloud upon his top, lakes, rivers, rocks, and precipices which were every way spread before me.

Joseph Craddock, An Account of some of the Most Romantic Parts of North Wales, London, 1777, p.15

32. Thomas Tudor, Cader Idris, *1802, pencil and wash on paper, 28.5 x 27.5, National Library of Wales, Aberystwyth*

33

James Ward, *Cader Idris on a Cloudy Day*, 1807, pen and ink wash drawing, 8.6 x 16.5, private collection

James Ward (1769-1859) was a London based professional artist who was originally trained as an engraver before taking up painting. He took lessons in anatomy to further his understanding. Subjects range from portraits, allegory and historical themes to animal pictures and landscapes. As a professional engraver Ward encountered a wide range of artists and he was also influenced by his brother in law, the painter George Morland. (1763-1804). In 1803 he saw a newly acquired Rubens at the National Gallery which impressed him with its rich colour. Ward was elected an associate of the Royal Academy in 1807 and an RA in 1811. He exhibited widely at both the British Institution and the Royal Academy.

Ward made sketching tours throughout Britain, usually in the summer months. He made two tours to north Wales, in 1802 and 1807. On both occasions he visited the celebrated "fasting woman of Tanyralt". Ward was fascinated by the subject and, in 1813, published a book about it. In 1811 Ward visited Gordale Scar near Malham in Yorkshire to make preliminary drawings for his large oil painting, *Gordale Scar* (1814, Tate Britain). It was commissioned by Lord Ribbesdale on whose land this natural feature is located. This painting is one of the key examples of the landscape sublime made in the nineteenth century. Ward had a long and successful career. He showed at the Academy for the last time in 1855. His work is represented in many public collections, National Gallery, Tate Britain, V&A, etc., in American institutions and in many private collections.

Cader Idris on a Cloudy Day was drawn by James Ward on an ascent of Cader Idris in September 1807. This atmospheric study depicts the dynamic power of nature with its swirling and obscuring clouds enveloping most of the view towards the mountain above Llyn-y-Cau. The profile of this vertical cliff edge is shown silhouetted against a streak of lighter sky. To the right can be seen the craggy slopes that lead up towards Mynydd Moel. This work has aspects of the sublime such as vastness, obscurity, grandeur and magnificence; the sense of awe and wonder before nature. There exists a line drawing by Ward taken from Richard Wilson's viewpoint that shows the whole cloudless vista towards Craig Cau with Llyn-y-Cau in its hollow below. It is fairly certain that Ward climbed the mountain on a number of occasions and the present sketch was made from close to the viewpoint chosen by Wilson for his view. By a combination of pen and wash Ward has been able to capture both the landscape structure and the fluidity of the transient clouds. This drawing was exhibited in the exhibition *Breadth & Quality: Oil Studies, Watercolours & Drawings by James Ward RA* held at the Lowell Libson Gallery, London in 2013.

33. James Ward, Cader Idris on a Cloudy Day, *1807, pen and ink wash drawing, 8.6 x 16.5, private collection*

34
Samuel Jackson, *Llyn-y-Cau, Cader Idris*, c.1833, watercolour on paper, 28 x 39, private collection

Samuel Jackson (1794–1869) was a professional artist and a leading member of the Bristol School of Artists. Primarily a watercolour artist he also worked in oil. During the mid eighteen-twenties he was commissioned to make a set of topographical watercolours of Bristol. He participated in the various exhibiting societies that emerged in Bristol from 1823 onwards and was elected to the Society of Painters in Watercolours based in London. During the 1830s Jackson made a number of visits to the mountainous regions of Britain. Scotland, the Lake District and Wales were chosen for mountain landscape subjects. He visited Switzerland during the 1850s and produced views of Alpine scenery. Jackson remained a prominent member of the artistic community of Bristol all his life.

In his watercolour *Llyn-y-Cau, Cader Idris*, Jackson presents a view of the lake and the vertical cliffs that rise above the enclosed pool. His viewpoint is much closer to Craig Cau than the one Wilson chose for his more expansive view. Jackson visited north Wales in 1829 and made a more extensive tour in 1833. This work is most likely to be derived from his later visit. In this view the mountain forms are partly obscured by the drifting clouds, particularly in the top right of the picture. This suggests aspects of the sublime, or at least the possibility of its intrusion into this serene scene. The use of colour in this work is exquisite. Jackson's juxtaposition of the complementary colours of blue and orange adds both light and beauty to the view. The white rocks in the foreground are illuminated by this effervescent light. There are no figures present in the picture, but some birds flying above the lake are a reassuring presence. In this composition there is little sky, emphasising the awesome scale of this location.

34. Samuel Jackson, Llyn-y-Cau, Cader Idris, *c.1833, watercolour on paper, 28 x 39, private collection*

35
David Cox, *Mountain Heights, Cader Idris*, 1850, watercolour over black chalk on paper, 47.8 x 74.6, National Gallery of Art, Washington

David Cox (1783–1859) was a professional artist and drawing master. He published four books on techniques for artists, the first in 1809 and the last in 1845. Initially he was an assistant scene-painter in various theatres before taking watercolour lessons from John Varley in 1804. Cox made his first visit to Wales in 1805 with the artist Charles Barber (1784–1854) and began to make his first watercolours that year. Subsequently Cox went on numerous sketching tours to the mountainous areas of Derbyshire, Yorkshire and to north Wales. Cox made several trips to the near continent; the first to Belgium and Holland in 1826. He had success with his watercolours in various exhibition societies and was elected to many of these bodies. He also exhibited at the Royal Academy regularly. From 1844 onwards Cox spent the summer months in Betws-y-coed, which he used as a base for excursions in search of mountain subjects. He made his last visit there in 1856; increasing ill-health curtailed further visits.

In 1850 David Cox made a large watercolour sketch showing a view on the summit ridge of Cader Idris. *Mountain Heights, Cader Idris* depicts the vista towards the summit peak of Pen-y-Gadair, which is hidden from view by the encroaching cloud. To the left of this area the profile of Craig Cau rises above the swirling cloud. This profile ridge that runs across the centre towards the left abruptly plunges to the valley below. It forms a silhouette against the vaporous sky, which is full of movement. This contrasts with the solidity of the immediate foreground area of rock and shale. This area gives a sense of security to the spectator as they contemplate the splendour of the view. His use of an alla-prima technique gives a freshness to the work, evoking the full effects of the weather; a treatment of subject unique to Cox. The colour is carefully orchestrated with the picture divided in half between cool and warm, the purples and blues contrasting with the sepia browns of the foreground areas. Cox wrote that, 'Sublime ideas are expressed by lofty and obscure images'; this sentiment found full expression in his watercolour *Mountain Heights, Cader Idris*.

35. David Cox, Mountain Heights, Cader Idris, *1850, watercolour over black chalk on paper, 47.8 x 74.6, National Gallery of Art, Washington*

36
Herbert Edwin Pelham Hughes-Stanton, *Cader Idris*, 1918, oil on canvas, 41.2 x 54.9, Royal Albert Memorial Museum, Exeter

Herbert Hughes-Stanton (1870–1937) was a landscape painter in watercolour and oil. He was taught by his father, the painter William Hughes (1842–1901). He exhibited at various London galleries including the Grosvenor and New Grafton galleries. He exhibited at the Royal Academy from 1897 onwards and was elected RA in 1919. Hughes-Stanton visited France from 1906, winning a gold medal at the Paris Salon two years running. He served as an Official War Artist during the Great War. His son Blair Hughes-Stanton (1902–1981) was a renowned wood engraver.

Herbert Hughes-Stanton made this oil painting of Cader Idris in 1918. It shows a view of the mountain seen from a vantage point close to Dolgellau. Looking to the south west the whole panorama of the mountain is visible. The three main peaks of the long ridge above the Mawddach estuary can be seen in this picture. They are firstly, Mynydd Moel, then the summit, Pen-y-Gadair, and finally, Mynydd Pencoed. Hughes-Stanton has applied the golden section compositional formula to his painting. The summit of Pen-y-Gadair adheres to this proportion. Other sub-divisions within the picture produce an accessible image, one that is very pleasing to the eye. This, combined with a sensitive use of naturalistic colour, adds to the painting's realism. The warm glow bathing the whole picture presents Cader Idris as a beautiful and non-threatening landscape. The wisps of cloud around the high peaks hint at the possibility that the weather could change. In the foreground a figure is shown walking towards a stile, leading the viewer through and into the picture.

36. Herbert Edwin Pelham Hughes-Stanton, Cader Idris, *1918, oil on canvas, 41.2 x 54.9, Royal Albert Memorial Museum, Exeter*

37
Tom Cross, *Cader Idris from Taly-Llyn*, 1994, watercolour and gouache on paper, 45.6 x 73.5, National Library of Wales, Aberystwyth

Tom Cross (1931-2009) was a professional artist, writer and lecturer. Cross studied painting at Manchester School of Art and then as a post-graduate student at the Slade School of Fine Art, from 1953 to 1956. During the period 1956–1963 he worked for the Welsh Arts Council in Cardiff. From 1963 to 1976 he taught Fine Art at Reading University. Tom Cross was Principal of Falmouth School of Art from 1976 to 1987 and wrote several books on art including, *Painting the Warmth of the Sun: St. Ives Artists, 1939–1975* (1984). He was primarily a landscape painter with a wide range of subjects including Cornwall, Wales and Italy. His work is represented in private and public collections in the UK and abroad.

Tom Cross painted this watercolour *Cader Idris from Taly-Llyn* in 1994. It is one of several views of the mountain that the artist has made. The first paintings of Cader Idris by Cross date from 1963 towards the end of his period at the Welsh Arts Council. Tom Cross has explored Cader Idris and made studies and paintings from various viewpoints on and around the mountain. These include views from the Dolgellau side and from high above Llyn-y-Cau. In *Cader Idris from Taly-Llyn*, Cross has made an individual choice of viewpoint. It is from high above the valley looking directly across to the bulk of Cader Idris. This vista looks westwards over the valley of Tal-y-llyn, the steep slopes of Mynydd Rugog intrude into the view on the left. There is no reassuring foreground present; instead a deep space gives the viewer a sense of insecurity. The colour in this work is fresh, naturalistic and direct. Cross has applied a robust and personal technique to evoke the feeling of the open air as experienced on the heights of a Welsh mountain.

37. Tom Cross, Cader Idris from Talyllyn, *1994, watercolour and gouache on paper, 54.6 x 73.5, National Library of Wales, Aberystwyth*

38
Pete Davis, Cader Idris, 1996, Selenium toned gelatin silver print, 38 x 56, private collection

Pete Davis (b.1947) is a Welsh photographer and lecturer who has produced a number of significant portfolios of photographic prints. Davis makes large format photographs which are presented as fine art in gallery exhibitions. Each show consists of a complete body of work which investigates the chosen subject fully in both visual form and historical context. In 1997 the exhibition *Cader Idris – Soul of a Lonely Place* was shown at the Museum of Modern Art Wales to much acclaim. The exhibition *Wildwood* at the Aberystwyth Art Centre in 2008 was the culmination of a long visual exploration of colour and form seen in nature. He was awarded a doctorate in fine art from Aberystwyth University in the following year. From 1998 he was the programme leader of the BA (Hons) Documentary Photography course, at the University of Wales, Newport. Pete Davis works from his house and studio at Alltyblaca. He participates in international conferences and gives talks and lectures at a number of Universities in the UK and abroad. His photographs are in a number of private and public collections in the UK and abroad.

The photograph, *Cader Idris* was taken from a high vantage point close to Mynydd Moel on the shoulder of Cader Idris. It is one of a portfolio of twenty prints made over a period of two years. The project involved twenty climbs of the mountain, in all weathers and seasons. These photographs were made using a large format camera which aids the process of slow, intense concentration on the topography and the prevailing atmospheric conditions. The viewpoint that Davis has chosen for this photograph is close to the one selected by Richard Wilson (1713 –1782) for his oil painting of 1765; its compositional structure features the same vertical mountain backdrop, the same rocky foreground and the same sense of height and grandeur.

38. Pete Davis, Cader Idris, *1996, Selenium toned gelatin silver print, 38 x 56, private collection*

39
Peter Bishop, *Cadair Idris and Llyn Cau*, 1996, mixed media drawing on paper, 58 x 82, National Library of Wales, Aberystwyth

Peter Bishop (b.1953) attended Banbury School of Art from 1970 to 1972. Then he studied painting at the Slade School of Fine Art graduating in 1975; his tutors included Bernard Cohen and Rita Donagh. In 1995 he obtained his Masters degree with distinction in the History of Art from the Birmingham Institute of Art and Design. In 2002 he completed his Doctorate at the School of Art, Aberystwyth University.

As an artist he has been making paintings since the early 1970s and held his first solo exhibition of Alpine landscapes in London in 1975. Since the mid 1980s he has concentrated on the mountains of Snowdonia as a subject for painting. He has held ten one-person shows and has exhibited in the Royal Academy's summer exhibitions and in many group shows. In 2012 he had a major exhibition on the theme of Cader Idris at the Museum of Modern Art Wales. His work is represented in many private and public collections.

Cadair Idris and Llyn Cau dates from 1996 and was exhibited at the Royal Academy summer show in 1997. It was made with reference to Richard Wilson's (1713 -1782) earlier painting of Cader Idris. This location was sometimes referred to as 'Wilson's Pool' by later visiting artists. The viewpoint for this drawing is from the path rising above the lake ascending to the summit. The work was made in the studio from sketches and notes made on the spot. By using a variety of drawing media the artist has been able to generate a range of abstracted marks that combine to form a recognisable image. The freedom of this approach allows the drawing to have its own identity - one that corresponds to the atmosphere of the location. In this view of lake and mountain the lack of sky, vertical cliffs and restricted colour all combine to evoke feelings of the sublime.

Llyn y Cau:

We now came to a second and more elevated lake, clear as glass and overlooked by steep cliffs in such a manner as to resemble the crater of a volcano.

Rev. J Evans, The Beauties of England and Wales, London, 1812, p.902.

39. Peter Bishop, Cadair Idris and Llyn Cau, *1996, mixed media drawing on paper, 58 x 82, National Library of Wales, Aberystwyth*

SIX
Pont Aberglaslyn: A Picturesque Viewpoint

An ancient bridge over the river Glaslyn set at the beginning of a steeply sided gorge would become a favoured subject for artists seeking a picturesque view in Snowdonia. The viewpoint chosen was either from the bridge itself, looking upstream, or from the steep bank that offered a view towards the bridge and the surrounding gorge. This location was highlighted in Thomas Pennant's *A Tour in Wales*, where it was reproduced from a watercolour by Moses Griffith. This engraving helped to establish the location, just south of Beddgelert, where accommodation could also be found for the visiting artists and tourists.

In the early pictures at this scenic location, there is a clear view up the gorge. As the eighteenth century merged into the nineteenth the view became obscured by increasing tree growth. Originally the bridge was on the edge of a tidal estuary. Attempts to claim Traeth Mawr from the sea reached their conclusion with the construction by William Madocks (1773–1828) of the causeway (The Cob) at Port Madock (Porthmadog). Begun in 1808, it was completed by 1811. Later, a storm breached the dyke and it was finally repaired in 1814. A consequence of this change of land use was that the environment around the bridge started to change from a coastal one to a pastoral one.

During the nineteenth century the pictorial views of Pont Aberglaslyn continued to follow the picturesque formula. The fashion for the picturesque with its tripartite compositional structure continued at this site. As the century advanced and the vegetation increased it became even more suited to this aesthetic treatment. The view towards the bridge began to disappear as a subject from the London exhibitions as the trees finally filled the valley above the bridge. This process was complete by the late 1860s. Today the view being photographed and reproduced in the Tourist Board literature is one of river and trees, with only a glimpse of the mountains beyond.

Pont Aberglaslyn described by Pennant:

The mountains approach so close, as to leave only room for the furious river to roll over its stony bed; above which is a narrow road, formed with incredible labour; impending over the water... The scenery is the most magnificent that can be imagined. The mountains rise to very uncommon height, and oppose to us nothing but a broken series of precipices, one above the other, high as the eye can reach.

Thomas Pennant, A Tour in Wales, vol.2., London, 1784, p.189.

Detail of Plate 42. Rev. William Henry Barnard, Pont Aberglaslyn

Plates 40-47

40

Samuel Hieronymus Grimm, *View of the Pass from Pont Aberglaslyn which divides Monmouth from Caernarvonshire,* **1780, engraving, 21.5 x 15, in Henry Penruddocke Wyndham,** *A Tour Through Monmouthshire and Wales,* **London, 1781, plate XI**

Samuel Hieronymus Grimm (1733–1794) was a Swiss artist who visited north Wales in the summer of 1777. He was employed to record a tour through part of north Wales. These drawings were published in 1781 to illustrate Henry Penruddocke Wyndham's (1736–1819) *A Tour though Monmouthshire and Wales*. It would soon be popular to engage a professional artist to join a tour party to make a visual record of their travels. Although Wyndham's book predates Pennant's *A Tour in Wales* by four years, it was not as influential as Pennant's more comprehensive publication of 1784.

This vertical picture by Samuel H Grimm depicts the view upstream from the bridge at Pont Aberglaslyn. It also shows the salmon net in the foreground and at left, the road to Beddgelert with a traveller making his way along it. This print was engraved from Grimm's original watercolour, made on the spot in 1777. Wyndham chose this image as a frontispiece for the second edition of *A Tour Through Monmouthshire and Wales*. Also included is a horizontal print titled *A View from below the Pont Aberglaslyn* (plate X). This viewpoint of mountain stream, bridge and gorge would soon become a favoured location for artists of the picturesque movement.

Pont Aberglaslyn

40. Samuel Hieronymus Grimm,
View of the Pass from Pont Aberglaslyn, *1780, engraving, 21.5 x 15,
in H P Wyndham*, A Tour Through Monmouthshire and Wales ...,
London, 1781, plate XI

Description of Pont Aberglaslyn adjacent to the picture by Grimm:

Here we paused, while the grandeur of the scenery before us, impressed a silent admiration on our senses. We, at length, moved slowly onwards, contemplating the wonderful chasm. An impending craggy cliff, at least eight hundred feet high, projects from every part of its broken front, stupendous rocks of the most capricious forms, and shadows a broad, translucid torrent, which rages, like a cataract, amid the huge ruins fallen from the mountain. On the opposite declivity, the disjointed fragments, crushing their mouldering props, seem scarcely prevented from overwhelming the narrow ridge, which forms the road on the brink of the flood.

H P Wyndham, A Tour through Monmouthshire and Wales, Salisbury, 1781, p.125.

41
Moses Griffith, attributed, *A Vignet of Pont Aber Glas Llyn*, engraving, 9 x 11, in Thomas Pennant, *A Tour in Wales*, The Journey to Snowdon, vol. 2, London, 1784, plate XI

Moses Griffith (1747–1809) was employed by the antiquary Thomas Pennant (1726–1798) from 1771 onwards to make topographical drawings and prints for his many books. He was born in north Wales and lived there. He produced a large number of watercolour views of country houses in a topographical manner. Griffith provided the majority of the pictures for Pennant's influential book, *A Tour in Wales*, published in its complete form in 1784.

A Vignet of Pont Aber Glas Llyn was inserted at the end of Pennant's *Journey to Snowdon* section in volume two of *A Tour in Wales*. This horizontal engraving has no plate signatures but it is almost certainly by Griffith. It depicts a view towards the bridge from the level of the river, with the bridge on the left and the mountains rising up behind. This is picturesque, the viewpoint is not set high, the composition is conventionally constructed and conforms to the golden mean, and there is plenty of sky in the top portion to negate any intrusion of the sublime. Pennant, like Wyndham, took care to have this plate placed adjacent to the text describing the bridge at Pont Aberglaslyn; this gives the tour guide narrative a visual status giving potential visitors an idea of what to expect at the location. The artist J. M. W. Turner (1775–1851) made a final tour to north Wales in 1799. Turner was familiar with the reproduction of this viewpoint in *A Tour in Wales* and made a vertical wash drawing in his sketchbook of the same view, but from a more elevated position.[6]

The bridge terminates the pass; and consists of a single arch, flung over a deep chasm, from rock to rock. Above is a considerable cataract, where the traveller at times may have much amusement, in observing the salmon, in great numbers, make their efforts to surpass the heights.

Thomas Pennant, *A Tour in Wales*, Vol. 2, London 1784, p.190.

Pont Aberglaslyn

41. Moses Griffith, attributed, A Vignet of Pont Aber Glas Llyn, *engraving, 9 x 11, in Thomas Pennant,* A Tour in Wales, The Journey to Snowdon, *vol. 2, London, 1784, plate XI*

42
Rev. William Henry Barnard, Pont *Aberglaslyn*, 1795, Graphite and watercolour on paper, 65.5 x 50, Tate Britain

William Henry Barnard (1767–1818) studied at Oxford University and, whilst there, took lessons in drawing from John Baptist Malchair (1729–1812), the Oxford-based musician, artist and drawing master. Malchair made several trips to north Wales to sketch mountain scenery in 1789, 1790 and in 1795, the same year as Barnard's wash drawing of Pont Aberglaslyn was made. Malchair's drawings of Welsh scenery are characterised by solid outlines and strong tonal washes. The application of monochrome washes to drawn lines were passed on to his pupils, such as Barnard, for use in their own drawings while visiting and recording landscape subjects.

This monochrome wash drawing shows a close-up view of the single-span bridge over the river Glaslyn from a slightly elevated viewpoint just below it. Pont Aberglaslyn is an important crossing point between Merionethshire and Caernarfonshire and in 1795, the year this work was made, the tidal waters of the estuary still came up to the bridge. In this view we can look beyond the bridge and up the narrow gorge, which is framed by steep-sided mountains. This open aspect would virtually disappear from later versions of this subject in the nineteenth century; increased tree growth was encouraged by the changes to the local environment caused by the reclaiming of hundreds of acres of land from the sea by the construction of Madock's dyke. The vertical format Barnard has chosen here allows for some exaggeration of height to the mountains, and this is further enhanced by the lack of sky. The technique of monochrome wash drawing on location was a favoured means of recording landscape at the end of the eighteenth century.

Pont Aberglaslyn described in verse by William Bingley:

The gloomy pass, where Aberglaslyn's arch
Yawns o'er the torrent. The disjointed crags
O'er the steep precipice in fragments vast...

William Bingley, North Wales, 1814, p.251

42. Rev. William Henry Barnard, Pont Aberglaslyn, *1795, Graphite and watercolour on paper, 65.5 x 50, Tate Britain*

43
Francis Nicholson, *Pont Aberglaslyn*, c. 1809, oil on canvas, 55.6 x 76, National Museum of Wales, Cardiff

Francis Nicholson (1753–1844) was a Yorkshire-based landscape artist in both watercolour and oil. Initially he painted portraits, sporting subjects and country house pictures. As he became more experienced, Nicholson specialised in landscape painting. These works were exhibited in London venues, such as the Royal Academy. He supplied many works for various publications such as Britton's *The Beauties of England and Wales* (1801–15). He moved to London in 1803 and, in 1804, was a founder member of the Society of Painters in Water Colours; a medium in which he excelled and was innovative. From 1816 onwards Nicholson became involved with new developments in lithography.

This oil painting *Pont Aberglaslyn*, is derived from a watercolour made on the spot. Nicholson had visited north Wales in 1800 and made an ascent of Cader Idris. The use of colour in this picture is naturalistic with none of the obscuring sublime present. In the watercolour version two figures are depicted and they are replicated in the oil painting. This may be for compositional reasons, to add local interest, or to give a sense of scale. The figures add to the picturesque effect as they survey the scene from their vantage point. From this position below the bridge can be seen the tidal waters of the estuary. Soon the tidal waters would be unable to reach the bridge and, by 1814, this attractive landscape feature would be lost. Nicholson's picture was engraved by Letitia Byrne (1779–1849) and published in 1809, the same year as the oil painting was completed.

43. Francis Nicholson, Pont Aberglaslyn, *c. 1809, oil on canvas, 55.6 x 76, National Museum of Wales, Cardiff*

44
David Cox, *Pont Aberglaslyn North Wales*, 1836, engraving, 9.8 x 14, in Thomas Roscoe, *Wanderings and Excursions in North Wales*, London and Birmingham, 1836, plate XXVIII, f.p. 204

David Cox (1783–1859) was a successful watercolour artist who specialised in painting mountain landscapes, particularly in Snowdonia. He was commissioned by Thomas Roscoe (1791–1871) to produce landscape watercolours for his travel book on north Wales. For *Wanderings and Excursions in North Wales* (1836) Roscoe commissioned five artists to make the illustrations specifically for reproduction in the guidebook. William Radclyffe (1789–1855) subsequently engraved these pictures and all fifty-one plates are of the highest quality. Cox provided thirty-one images for the north Wales book. A number of these are mountain views and reflect Cox's developing knowledge of, and expertise in recording, Welsh mountain scenery.

The engraving *Pont Aberglaslyn North Wales* faithfully reproduces Cox's picture and illustrates one of the views that had become established for this location. In this version Cox has placed the bridge in the centre of the composition. The lightest area of sky in the distance immediately above the intruding mountain on the left gives atmosphere to the scene as well as retaining topographical accuracy. On the right side of the picture shown in a mid grey tone the high mountains meet and mingle with the clouds. Cox would often use a contrast of a lighter sky tone set against a mountain profile, particularly in his more sublime paintings of Snowdonia's mountain scenery. Cox has shown more figures in this picture than Nicholson did in his earlier painting suggesting, perhaps, the increasing popularity of this site as a picturesque location.

44. David Cox, Pont Aberglaslyn North Wales, *1836, engraving, 9.8 x 14, in Thomas Roscoe,* Wanderings and Excursions in North Wales, *London and Birmingham, 1836, plate XXVIII, f.p. 204*

45
Myles Birket Foster. *Pont Aberglaslyn*, c.1858, engraving, 12.7 x 8, in Black's *Picturesque Guide to North Wales*, Edinburgh, 1886, f p. 130

The artist Myles Birket Foster (1825–1899) contributed a view looking upstream towards Pont Aberglaslyn that is the epitome of the picturesque. This picture was for Charles and Adam Black's guide book. Black's *Picturesque Guide to North Wales* was published in various editions from 1851 onwards. Black's guides were increasingly designed for the railway age, and this edition, dated 1886, contained a comprehensive and detailed map of north Wales. Foster was a favourite artist of Queen Victoria. He understood the public taste and was able to supply it.

By the last decades of the nineteenth century the public taste was for a more sentimental approach to the treatment of landscape. In the engraving, *Pont Aberglaslyn*, Foster had found an ideal picturesque subject. In this vertical picture can be seen the bridge with two visitors, and beyond them, through the arch, the rocks of the salmon-leap in the stream bed. The river is shown in a very placid, low-water state. The exaggeration in the mountains' height, particularly beyond the bridge on the left, is so great that it negates a feature that would usually increase ideas of a sublime nature. In the picture the mountains reveal weaknesses of drawing of topographic structure, and this further enhances the picturesque imagery of the overall piece. The sky is equally calm and placid, the summer day equivalent of a classical treatment which allows the idealised clouds to recede in diminishing bands of perspective.

Pont Aberglaslyn viewpoint in the mid 1880's:

... we reach a scene that has occupied the artist's pencil perhaps more than any other in North Wales; the far-famed bridge over the Glaslyn. No words can describe the rich beauty of this attractive spot. The road suddenly narrows into a pass overhung with perpendicular rocks on one side; and the pines give quite an Alpine tinge to the scene.

Askew Roberts, The Gossiping Guide, London and Oswestry, 1883, p.194

45. Myles Birket Foster. Pont Aberglaslyn, *c.1858, engraving, 12,7 x 8, in Black's* Picturesque Guide to North Wales, *Edinburgh, 1886, f p. 130*

46
Benjamin Williams Leader, *The Pass of Aberglaslyn*, 1871, oil on canvas, 56 x 48, Dudley Museum and Art Gallery, (Dudley Museum Services)

Benjamin Williams Leader (1831–1923) was a landscape painter who was born in Worcester. After study at the Worcester School of Design he moved to London in 1854 to study at the Royal Academy. In the same year he exhibited his first painting in the annual summer exhibition held each year at the Academy. This early success enabled him to embark on his career as a painter of landscape subjects. He changed his name from Benjamin Leader Williams to Benjamin Williams Leader to avoid confusion with other artists with the surname Williams. His subjects included the river valleys of Worcestershire and the Severn, along with views in Wales and Scotland. Early patronage enabled him to make a considerable fortune from the sales of his work, and he showed at the Academy every year from 1854 until 1922. Many of his paintings show some aspect of human activity in the landscape, and this contributed to their popularity with a broad range of admirers and patrons. His naturalistic landscapes were often depicted in the sunshine of early evening and this gave many pictures a golden, glowing range of colours. He moved to Surrey in 1889 purchasing a house designed by Norman Shaw (1831–1912) the Scottish architect.

The Pass of Aberglaslyn is an oil painting, dating from 1871 and shows the encroaching tree growth on the left that is beginning to restrict the view upstream. Leader has used a vertical format for his view and this emphasises the picturesque aspects of the scene. The river is tumbling over some large boulders in the stream bed and pine trees descend to the water's edge on the left. The view beyond the middle distance is restricted by the large bulk of mountain form which comes into view from the right. This painting fits the tripartite compositional formula promoted by William Gilpin to produce a picturesque effect in a picture. Leader has used a range of soft muted hues, creating a slightly gloomy effect of light that is often a feature of deep gorges in Wales. At the very top of the picture is a small area of blue sky emerging from the obscuring clouds, implying an improving prospect in the weather conditions to come. The range of restricted brownish colour produces a natural realism associated with Leader's treatment of landscape scenery.

46. Benjamin Williams Leader, The Pass of Aberglaslyn, *1871*, oil on canvas, 56 x 48, Dudley Museum and Art Gallery, (Dudley Museum Services)

47
Russell Gilder, *A View from Pont Aberglaslyn*, 2014, 144 x 104, charcoal on paper, private collection

Russell Gilder (b.1966) is a professional landscape painter whose subject matter is derived from the forests and woods of the borderland of England and Wales. Mortimer Forest in south Shropshire is one location the artist has explored in both drawing and large scale oil paintings. Gilder's landscape paintings often refer to the arcadian forests and mountainous vistas associated with these historic landscapes. These paintings are both real and imagined, with the arcadian aspect underpinning their visual identity. Gilder attended the London College of Printing and completed a design foundation course in 1985. He later studied at the School of Art, Shrewsbury College, completing the foundation art and design course there in 1993. He studied painting at Birmingham School of Art graduating with a fine art honours degree in 1996. In 2001 he completed a postgraduate course at the University of Greenwich, London. Gilder has exhibited widely including in the Royal Academy's summer exhibition and has received many awards and prizes in both drawing and painting. He lives in south west England, working from his studio in Devon. His work is in private and public collections in the UK and abroad.

A View from Pont Aberglaslyn is a vertical charcoal drawing dating from 2014. In this large monochrome drawing we are presented with an image of water and foliage. The trees fill the gorge encroaching to the rivers edge and in the far distance the profile of high mountains can be seen above the trees. This composition adheres to the picturesque conventions of the site but is now presented in a contemporary manner. The technique used by the artist in this charcoal drawing, with its vigour of marks and strong tonal values, creates a powerful evocation of place that is the hallmark of Russell Gilders art. The viewpoint used by Gilder looking up the Glaslyn river from Pont Aberglaslyn was originally drawn by S H Grimm in the 1770s when the view upstream still retained its open aspect.

Bingley on the Pont Aberglaslyn viewpoint:

The varied scene beyond the bridge of wood, rock and vale, is extremely fine from several stations. The mountains huge appear emergent, and their broad bare backs upheave into the clouds; their tops ascend the sky.

William Bingley, North Wales, London, 1814, p.254

Pont Aberglaslyn

47. *Russell Gilder,* A View from Pont Aberglaslyn, *2014, 144 x 104, charcoal on paper, private collection*

SEVEN
Llyn Idwal: A Sublime Viewpoint

As a subject for painting, Llyn Idwal appeared comparatively late. Even though it was described in text as early as Pennant's *A Tour in Wales* (1784), it was not generally depicted until the third decade of the nineteenth century. In 1836 an engraved version of this subject, originally drawn by David Cox, appeared in Thomas Roscoe's guidebook on North Wales. The compositional structure applied by Cox to this view of Llyn Idwal is sublime, characterised by a barrier motif of vertical rocks rising directly above the lake, which results in a reduced area for the depiction of sky.

This viewpoint is only accessible on foot and is located half a mile from the Ogwen Falls Bridge in the Nant Ffrancon valley. This site consists of a mountain lake trapped in a hollow, below a barrier of mountains which rise up vertically all around it. This enclosed viewpoint did not fit the accepted visual processes that artists had applied to other viewpoints in Snowdonia, such as at Pont Aberglaslyn, or to the view of Snowdon from Capel Curig. The geographical structures at this location perfectly met the requirements of artists seeking the 'horror and immensity' of Edmund Burke's sublime. This viewpoint soon became associated with generating the effects of the sublime with artists and tourists alike. The fact that the weather was often inclement produced another ingredient of the sublime: obscurity. The first painting shown at the Royal Academy of this subject was *Llyn Idwal near Capel Curig* by William Fowler (1796–1870) in 1840.

From this time onwards the Llyn Idwal site supplied artists with a ready made view of lake and mountains whose summits were often hidden and dramatically obscured by cloud. The pursuit of cloud-covered mountains could also be satisfied at other nearby locations such as Tryfan (918 m) with its distinctive pointed shape. Artists applied their own interpretations to the barrier motif seen at the Idwal viewpoint. This location and the Nant Ffrancon area has continued to be a favoured one for the representation of the mountain sublime in Snowdonia.

Llyn Idwal as described by Pennant:

It was a fit place to inspire murderous thoughts, environed with horrible precipices, shading a lake, lodged in its bottom, The shepherds fable, that it is the haunt of Demons; and that no bird dare fly over its damned water...

Thomas Pennant, *A Tour in Wales*, vol. 2., London, 1784, p.162

Detail of Plate 48. George Fennel Robson, The Devil's Kitchen

Plates 48-57

48
George Fennel Robson, *The Devil's Kitchen, Llyn Idwal, North Wales*, c.1830, watercolour, 19.9 x 27.2, Whitworth Art Gallery, Manchester

George Fennel Robson (1788-1833) was a gifted watercolour artist who specialised in Scottish mountain scenery. In Durham he had taken lessons in drawing and in 1806 he moved to London to pursue his vocation where he received advice on watercolour technique from John Varley (1778-1842). From 1807 he exhibited at the Royal Academy and at a number of other exhibiting societies. In 1814 he published a set of forty etchings of Scottish mountain views with the title *Scenery of the Grampians*. John Ruskin was an admirer of Robson's skills, especially his use of colour in his mountain pictures. He was a very successful artist who enjoyed patronage from many of the leading collectors of the day including Walter Fawkes (1769-1825) of Farnley Hall an early patron of J M W Turner.

When Robson arrived at the Llyn Idwal site on a visit to north Wales in the early 1830s it was a subject that was rarely depicted. However Robson, with his experience of painting mountain scenery in Scotland, saw its visual potential as a vehicle for the expression of the sublime aesthetic.

Robson's *Devil's Kitchen Llyn Idwal North Wales* shows the enclosed lake and its mountain backdrop forming a visual barrier that denies pictorial space. It is more sublime than picturesque, with the lack of any figures highlighting the site's isolation. The low viewpoint and lack of sky emphasise the sense of awe associated with the Idwal site.

In the title of this watercolour there is a reference to the 'Devil's Kitchen', a feature of the location that Pennant had pointed out. He wrote 'It is a horrible gap, in the centre of a great black precipice, extending in length about a hundred and fifty yards; in depth, about a hundred; and only six wide; perpendicularly open to the surface of the mountain'.[7]

A watercolour titled, *Llyn Idwal North Wales – Twilight* was exhibited by Robson at the OWCS in 1831. David Cox saw Robson's picture at the OWCS and then added this site to his north Wales subjects.

John Ruskin on Robson's mountain subjects such as Llyn Idwal:

... for the sake of the nature, not the picture, and therefore, having this germ of true life, it grew and throve. Robson did not paint purple hills because he wanted to show how he could lay on purple; but because he truly loved their dark peaks.

John Ruskin, *Modern Painters*, vol.3., London, 1856, p.345

48. *George Fennel Robson,* The Devil's Kitchen, Llyn Idwal, North Wales, *c.1830, watercolour, 19.9 x 27.2, Whitworth Art Gallery, Manchester*

49
David Cox, *Llyn Idwal*. 1836, engraving, 9.8 x 14, in Thomas Roscoe, *Wanderings and Excursions in North Wales*, London and Birmingham, 1836, plate XXIII

This view of Llyn Idwal was reproduced in Roscoe's guidebook to north Wales published in 1836. Here David Cox (1783–1859) promotes the sublime merits of this site over the picturesque. Roscoe's book was lavishly illustrated by artists he commissioned and helped to maintain the established viewpoints. It also gave visual identity to lesser-known sites such as the viewpoint at Llyn Idwal. This engraving based on the original watercolour makes full use of the print medium's capability to produce deep velvety blacks, and these are allowed to dominate the view. The viewer is presented with the deep grand gloom that is often a feature of Cox's vision of mountain scenery.

In this picture are some wild-looking goats silhouetted against the dark and forbidding-looking lake. A lone bird is shown flying across the lake, which is represented light against dark, its lack of height above the water contributing to the viewer's sense of isolation within this vast mountain arena. The vertical stream running straight down from the mountain heights of Glyder Fawr and Y Garn to the bottom of the Idwal Slabs shows up as a streak of light tone against the darker mountainside beyond the lake. The image that Cox presents perfectly matches the written description by Roscoe.

Roscoe on the atmosphere of the Llyn Idwal site:

I was particularly struck with the bleak and stormy character of the scenery around Lake Idwal, singularly situated in a hollow of the mountain summit. Restless as the sea, and fiercely swept by the autumnal blasts, as I passed the lone and savage spot, its aspect fell chill upon the spirits ...

Thomas Roscoe, North Wales, 1836, p.159

49. David Cox, Llyn Idwal, *1836, engraving, 9.8 x 14, in Thomas Roscoe,* Wanderings and Excursions in North Wales, *London and Birmingham, 1836, plate XXIII*

50
Samuel Jackson, *Llyn Idwal, Snowdonia*, c.1835, watercolour, 20.8 x 31.1, Fitzwilliam Museum, Cambridge

Bristol based artist Samuel Jackson (1794–1869) made a sketching tour to north Wales in 1833 and *Llyn Idwal, Snowdonia* was painted a few years later. Jackson's watercolour is taken from the same viewpoint as Robson and Cox. It is evocative of the atmospheric conditions found at this site.

In this watercolour of Llyn Idwal, we are confronted with a barrier motif running across the whole composition from left to right. On the right the sky is obliterated altogether by the towering rock that rises vertically from the lake at a point where it is hidden behind a large boulder sitting menacingly in the foreground. The treatment of light also enables a sublime reading of the image to be made. Jackson has applied a particular method of working to this view of Llyn Idwal; one that enables the picture to be built up by a process of diffused watercolour washes that are also dabbed and scratched away from the surface to allow highlights to exist minutely. The result of this process is to present an image that is to a degree, out of focus. This aspect of its obscurity produces the sublime rather than the picturesque. The solid forms of the mountains are now reduced to a transient spectacle seen through the subdued light of dawn that now is only illuminating the surrounding high peaks. It is not a topographical picture of mountain structure. Jackson has severely restricted his use of colour in this work and this contributes to the sublime mood that pervades the entire picture. In *Llyn Idwal, Snowdonia* the artist has used a predominantly grey-green combination of colours for the mountain and lake. These are offset by the pale intermingled tints of the yellowish and blue colours of the sky. Also in this part, the vibrant light of the dawn breaks in from the left side of the picture and this allows a range of lighter hues to be present on the mountain summits where they make contact with the sky. The absence of any figures or animals in this painting further enhances the sublime aspect that Jackson is presenting to the viewer in his picture of Llyn Idwal.

50. Samuel Jackson, Llyn Idwal, Snowdonia, *c.1835, watercolour, 20.8 x 31.1, Fitzwilliam Museum, Cambridge*

51
Edward Pugh, *Nant Ffrancon*, c.1813, aquatint, 14.8 x 20, in Edward Pugh, *Cambria Depicta*, London, 1816, f.p.106

Edward Pugh (1763–1813) of Ruthin, made a watercolour of Nant Francon based on his travels through Snowdonia and it was reproduced in aquatint in his book on north Wales. As Pugh made clear in the title of his book, *Cambria Depicta: A Tour through North Wales Illustrated with Picturesque Views By a Native Artist* he emphasised his Welsh credentials. This gave his volume a greater status compared with the slim volumes published by English visitors. It was the most significantly influential book since Pennant's *A Tour in Wales.* Pugh's *Cambria Depicta* was published posthumously in 1816.

In the Nant Francon aquatint print Pugh shows the sweep of the new road through the pass against the backdrop of the highest mountains in Snowdonia. In this picture can be seen the apparent ease with which visitors could travel through this region of north Wales, on the metalled road, as they can still do today, on the A5. In Pugh's wild and desolate picture two figures can be seen on the road at the bottom left, a gentleman who is pointing to the scenery for his lady companion to enjoy, whilst on the right, underneath the mountain backdrop, can be seen a coach with two horses. Pugh wrote that visitors would be 'delighted with the sublimity of the scenery all the way down Nant Ffrancon, because the western side of it is by much the grandest'.[8] Pugh did not illustrate the nearby Tryfan: instead he gave instructions as to where an artist should stand to see the dominating profile of the mountain.

Edward Pugh's advice on viewpoints in Nant Ffrancon (Tryfan):

I would advise the artist to get to the north side of Ogwen lake, and up the heights, till he can suit himself with points to his mind; assuring him that Llyn Idwal, with other grand objects, come in very boldly, and if he is so lucky as to be favoured with a murky sky, still clear enough to get the contour of the mountain and rocks, he will not be disappointed. As the new road on the north side of the river is finished, travellers, in this track, will be much more delighted with the sublimity of the scenery all the way down Nant Ffrancon because the western side of it is by much the grandest...

Edward Pugh, Cambria Depicta, London, 1816, pp.109 -110

51. *Edward Pugh,* Nant Ffrancon, *c.1813, aquatint, 14.8 x 20, in Edward Pugh,* Cambria Depicta, *London, 1816, f.p.106*

52
Alfred William Hunt, *Cwm Trifaen, The Track of an Ancient Glacier*, 1857-8, oil on canvas, 60.3 x 90.8, Tate Britain, London

Alfred William Hunt (1830–1896) was inspired by reading Roscoe's North Wales guide and he knew the work of David Cox well. He made his first tour to north Wales in 1856, the same year that John Ruskin published his fourth volume of *Modern Painters*, subtitled *Of Mountain Beauty*, returning there the following year. He also had an affinity with the new methods employed by the Pre-Raphaelite painters whose works he had seen at the Royal Academy in the 1850s. All these influences were assimilated into his working methods in both watercolour and oil.

This oil painting dates from around 1857. In the title Hunt acknowledges Ruskin's influence by quoting from Ruskin. Hunt has borrowed the phrase 'the tracks of ancient glaciers' from *Modern Painters*.[9] In *Trifaen, The Track of an ancient Glacier*, Hunt presents a more expressive view of the wild mountain landscape, with the obscured peaks of Tryfan appearing as a dark silhouette at the top right of the picture. The mountain ridge that Hunt has depicted in the upper portion of the picture acts as a barrier within the composition and this restricts the amount of recessional space that can be seen. In this painting, the viewer is suspended above a deep space consisting of rock strata before the eye is led across to the mountains beyond. As with other sublime representations of this site there is very little sky present. The atmospheric and stormy weather effects shown by Hunt are a visual equivalent to Roscoe's text description. Although this work retains an element of Cox's treatment of weather, with swirling clouds and darkening sky, there is also evidence of a Pre-Raphaelite influence. This accurate treatment can be seen in the painting of the rocks in the foreground and the middle distance, along with their associated mountain forms. Hunt's technique reveals the particular geology of the site. The treatment of light is harsh, with a marked contrast between those parts in shadow and those in bright sunshine.

52. *Alfred William Hunt*, Cwm Trifaen, The Track of an Ancient Glacier, *1857-8, Oil on canvas, 60.3 x 90.8, Tate Britain, London*

53
Charles William Mansel Lewis, *The Devil's Kitchen, Llyn Idwal*, 1882, oil on canvas, 97 x 184, Stradey Castle collection, Llanelli

Charles William Mansel Lewis (1845–1931) was a Welsh landscape painter and artist of social realism whose works were often set in the countryside in and around his estate at Stradey Castle, near Llanelli in south Wales. He was educated at Eton College where he was taught drawing and introduced to art by the father and son team of Sam and William Evans. At Oxford University Mansel Lewis read classics and became friendly with the drawing master, William Rivière, from whom he commissioned a painting. He also purchased some work from his son, Briton Rivière. In 1872 he inherited the Stradey House estate and he met another artist, Hubert Von Herkomer (1849–1914), a year later, when he came to give advice on the house refurbishments and construction of an artist's studio. The house was then renamed Stradey Castle. At this time Mansel Lewis also began to purchase work from Herkomer. They became good friends and the two of them decided to explore landscape painting together. Between 1879 and 1884 they made camping trips lasting up to two months to north Wales in search of mountain landscape subjects. In 1879, whilst camping at the Llyn Idwal site, Herkomer made several prints on a portable etching press. In Snowdonia, both artists used a plein air approach on large canvasses, with an emphasis on carefully observed geological structure, and used a restricted colour palette of muted browns and contrasts of light and dark. Mansel Lewis was a member of the Royal Society of Painter-Etchers and exhibited sixteen works in the London exhibitions between 1872 and 1882 including nine at the Royal Academy. Paintings by Mansel Lewis, Herkomer and others are in the collections at Stradey Castle.

This large oil painting titled, *The Devil's Kitchen* was exhibited at the Royal Academy in 1882 and is the only painting of Welsh mountain scenery that Mansel Lewis exhibited there. We are presented with a view of high mountains encircling the unseen lake at Llyn Idwal in north Wales. The term, *Devil's Kitchen* is mentioned by Pennant in *A Tour in Wales* (1784) and refers to a deep crevice that cuts into the cliff face above the lake. In this rectangular painting the mountains are shown silhouetted against the lighter sky from the centre to the right of the painting. On the left, the highest mountains are hidden by the obscuring cloud, masking their profiles from view and producing a sublime image. These mountains are shown in very deep shadow and the use of browns and muted orange hues heighten the sublime aesthetic further. A thin streak of sunlight cuts across the top of the foreground ridge where a number of sheep can be seen, but no people are present. The immediate foreground is also in shadow caused by the darkening clouds overhead. A thin patch of sunlight can be seen above this foreground area and this compositionally links this foreground with the dark mountains beyond. The visual power of this work is enhanced by the contrasts of light and dark. A companion painting dating from the same period, titled *Snowdonia*, is also in the Stradey Castle collection. It shows a view across Nant Ffrancon from a high viewpoint close to Llyn Idwal with the distinctive triangular shape of Tryfan in the distance.

53. Charles Mansel Lewis, The Devil's Kitchen, Llyn Idwal, *1882, oil on canvas, 97 x 184, Stradey Castle Collection, Llanelli.*

54
John Piper, *Cwm Idwal*, 1949, ink, watercolour and charcoal on paper, 21.6 x 27.9, private collection

John Piper (1903–1992) arrived in Nant Ffrancon in 1943 whilst working as an official war artist. He returned regularly over the following years staying in rented cottages in and around the Nant Ffrancon valley. Unlike the casual visitors, Piper was resident for several months at a time. This meant that he was able to explore the area fully as Pennant had done in the eighteenth century. Many of Piper's works from this period in Snowdonia display restricted and sombre use of colour. This may reflect the desolate nature of the terrain or the scarcity of available art materials caused by the war.

Piper's *Cwm Idwal* was made from a sketch drawn on the spot from a position below and to the right of the enclosed lake. He presents a close-up view of the cliff face seen rising above the lake. On the top right can be seen the narrow gulley known as the 'Devils Kitchen' or '*Twll Ddu*' [the black hole]. The foreground rocks are carefully observed and reflect Piper's interest in geology and his fascination with the way rock can change colour according to the light and season. Piper's *Cwm Idwal* follows the same conventions that were originally applied by artists at this viewpoint in the mid nineteenth century. Piper uses a barrier format that denies conventional pictorial space. This feature, along with the narrow strip of sky at the top of the image adds to the sublime effect. Piper also visited the nearby Tryfan and other mountains from his various bases in the Nant Ffrancon area.

A guidebook description of Llyn Idwal:

Llyn Idwal, a gloomy lake in a hollow backed by the steep sides of Glyder Fawr... If you have your choice of days, and can afford to brave the weather, choose a day when the clouds are scudding about the mountains to see Idwal, and then you will certainly remember it.

Askew Roberts, *The Gossiping Guide to Wales*, London, 1883, p.188

54. *John Piper,* Cwm Idwal, *1949, ink, watercolour and charcoal on paper, 21.6 x 27.9, private collection*

55
Kyffin Williams, *Tryfan 2*, c.1981, oil on canvas, 50 x 110, Atkinson Art Gallery Collection, Southport

Kyffin Williams (1918-2006) was a Welsh painter whose subject matter was the landscape of north Wales and portraits of the people who lived there. He received his art training at the Slade School of Fine Art,1941–1944, then temporarily housed in Oxford. In 1973 he was able to give up his part-time teaching position in Highgate school, London and moved to north Wales to live and paint. From his base in Anglesey Kyffin Williams explored the mountain scenery of Snowdonia, visiting the highest peaks particularly around Snowdon itself. This produced a range of subjects from studies of the stark mountains to sensitive portraits of the local farmers.

Tryfan 2 depicts the mountain, Tryfan, as seen from above the Nant Ffrancon pass. The bold triangular silhouette of Tryfan is seen against the snow-covered ridge behind. This wide panorama view presents a vista of upland Snowdonia by an artist who had explored the area fully. Using a palette of restricted colour, greys and muted whites, the barren atmosphere of the high mountains is perfectly captured in this work. The placing of Tryfan slightly off-centre contributes to an awkwardness of feeling related to the difficulty of actually getting to this viewpoint. Many of Kyffin Williams' paintings of Tryfan and nearby Snowdon are characterised by a close-up compositional formula and a monochrome palette. The largest public collection of his work is at the National Library of Wales, Aberystwyth.

Roscoe's description of Tryfan seen from the heights of Glyder Fawr:

The surface of the ground upon which I stood, – the summit of the Glyder Fawr, – had a most singular appearance. It seemed as if had been been washed by a tremendous sea; the stones lay loose, and strewn at hazard as on some wild coast; the rocks, bare, cloven, and jagged, lay crossing each other in different directions; while the huge, pointed Trifaen, with its sharp, angular projections, height above height, seemed like some huge monster... with naked peaks that reared their grey crests to the clouds.

Thomas Roscoe, North Wales, London, 1836, pp.158-159

Llyn Idwal 145

55. *Kyffin Williams, Tryfan 2, c.1981,*
oil on canvas, 50 x 110,
Atkinson Art Gallery Collection Southport

56
Peter Prendergast, *Nant Ffrancon Valley, Summer*, 1990, oil on canvas, 135 x 283, Bangor University collection

Peter Prendergast (1946-2007) was born in south Wales and attended Cardiff School of Art. He later trained at the Slade School of Fine Art from 1964 to1967. This was followed a year later by an MA in painting at Reading University. In 1969 he moved to Bethesda with his wife Lesley to live and work. The village was close to the Penrhyn Quarry, which became an important subject for the artist. Snowdonia and its mountain scenery were also close by and became the subject of many paintings. He often applied his paint using an impasto technique with a much stronger use of colour than that used by Kyffin Williams. He was able to handle the demands of the larger canvas and these works have a monumental grandeur and compositional strength that met the demands of such a 'large' subject. At the time of his death in 2007 he left behind a significant body of work. His work is represented in both private and public collections in Britain and abroad.

Nant Ffrancon Valley, Summer, one of a series of paintings was painted in the artist's studio from visual notes and drawings made on location. The broad sweep of the valley is shown with two enclosing areas of mountain on each side of the composition. This leads the eye into and through to the background: a compositional formula that William Gilpin used and artists applied to their picturesque views such as those at Pont Aberglaslyn. In this painting Prendergast has used the full range of prismatic colour available. He has brought to the scene the colours of the spectrum and applied them to a view that can often be regarded as bleak – especially when cloud fills the valley. It is his personal joy in the use of colour and his expressive brush strokes that give the viewer such an evocation of place.

56. Peter Prendergast Nant Ffrancon Valley, Summer, *1990, oil on canvas, 135 x 283, Bangor University Collection.*

57
David Woodford, *Cwm Idwal from Ffynnon Lloer*, 2008 – 2013, oil on board, 77 x 113, collection of the artist

David Woodford (born 1938 in Yorkshire) spent his formative years at Church Stretton where the Welsh mountains spill into Shropshire. He trained at the West Sussex College of Art 1955–1959 and at Leeds College of Art 1959–1960. Later he attended the Royal Academy Schools in London, graduating from there in 1968. After leaving the Academy he moved to Wales and lived at Dinas Mawddwy for the next three years. In 1971 he moved to the Nant Ffrancon area of north Wales so he could concentrate on painting the mountain landscape of Snowdonia as a professional artist. He has been a member of the Royal Cambrian Academy since 1977 and was awarded a Gold Medal for Fine Art at the National Eisteddfod in 1983. His landscapes in watercolour and in oil reveal the diversity of his mountain subject matter usually acquired fairly close to his home in Bethesda. Although he works within the realist tradition and his paintings are keenly observed from nature, he intends his work to be regarded by its abstract condition as much as its topographical content. His works are in private collections and national collections including the National Museum of Wales and the National Library of Wales.

Cwm Idwal from Ffynnon Lloer is an oil painting that the artist has worked on for a number of years in his studio in the Nant Ffrancon pass. It embodies much of the truth-to-nature philosophy that John Ruskin had originally proposed for use by landscape painters. In David Woodford's hands we get a lot more than Ruskin's dictum; the painting displays an intensely observed passion for the wild mountain landscape, a landscape that Woodford has explored on foot and recorded in drawings and colour studies in all weathers and climatic conditions over many years. In this painting he is able to emphasise a range of colour that is not always apparent to the casual observer. The painting radiates a magical light from within, giving a transient quality characteristic of this part of Snowdonia.

57. *David Woodford*, Cwm Idwal from Ffynnon Lloer, *2008 - 2013, oil on board, 77 x 113, collection of the artist*

EIGHT
Arenig Fawr: A Painter's Mountain

Arenig Fawr (854 metres) is the highest of the Arenig range and is situated six miles from Bala close to the A4212 road and within the Snowdonia National Park. The area also includes several other peaks and lakes such as Llyn Celyn. It was in the early twentieth century that the Arenigs became a subject for landscape painting. This location was first painted by the Welsh artist James Dickson Innes (1887–1914), who persuaded two artist friends he had met through the Slade School of Fine Art to join him at the site. These were Augustus John (1878–1961), a fellow Welsh artist, and the Australian Derwent Lees (1885–1931). For a period of two years from 1911 to 1913 the artists made small landscapes in the post impressionist style. They were painted in the open air on wooden panels, reminiscent of the Welsh eighteenth century artist Thomas Jones (1742–1803). The recent exposure of post-impressionism was a liberating influence on these artists and the application of a Fauve-like palette was now applied to this sombre subject. The use of bright colour is offset by its application in a tonal manner, offering a unique blend of the two.

The area is more remote today than it was when the 24-year-old Innes arrived in the winter of 1910 to 1911. In those days the location was served by the Bala–Ffestiniog railway, and there was a request stop at Arenig Halt. A pub was close by (now a private house), where Innes initially stayed. Thereafter Innes and John rented a small cottage, 'Nant-Ddu', and Lees joined them later. The so-called Arenig School flourished for two years with Innes and John contributing the majority of the mountain landscapes. These paintings are highly regarded today, and represent a particular kind of British eccentricity similar to that found in Samuel Palmer's (1805–1881) Shoreham period with its intensity of artistic vision.

The remoteness of the Arenigs did not attract many artists again until the painter and poet Clyde Holmes (1940–2008) came to live at an old farmhouse at the head of the Cwm Hesgin valley in 1971. From this isolated spot he was able to paint the varying moods and patterns of light and dark caused by the cloud formations he observed on the southern uplands of Snowdonia.

Arenig described by Borrow as barren and treeless:

Arenig is certainly barren enough, for there is neither tree or shrub upon it, but there is something majestic in its huge bulk. Of all the hills which I saw in Wales none made a greater impression upon me.

George Borrow, Wild Wales, London, 1862, p. 287

Detail of Plate 63. Clyde Holmes, Billowing Cloud, Snowdonia

Plates 58-63

58

James Dickson Innes, *Arenig*, 1911, ink and watercolour on paper, 25.4 x 35.6, Tate Britain

James Dickson Innes (1887–1914) was a Welsh landscape painter, born in Llanelli. He studied at Carmarthen Art School and then at the Slade School of Fine Art in London from 1905 to 1908. It was while at the Slade he met Derwent Lees (1885–1931) and Ian Strang (1886–1952). In 1907 he met the older painter, Augustus John (1878–1961), a fellow-Welshman. Innes made painting excursions to Collioure in southern France where Matisse and Derain had painted, in 1908 and again in 1911. These landscape paintings of Collioure and its surrounding mountain scenery were successful both artistically and in monetary terms. He first visited Arenig late in 1910 on the rebound from a love affair with Euphemia Lamb (1886–1957), an artist's model and part of the mileau around Augustus John. Innes is said to have buried a silver casket of her love letters on the summit of Arenig Fawr. The 1910 visit was inspirational for Innes and he began developing his quick impulsive alla prima landscapes of Arenig and the surrounding mountain vistas. These works were painted on the spot in strong hues yet retaining the tonal values associated with the location. Many were painted on small wooden panels that were easily portable so that several could be carried around and used at different locations in the landscape. His friends Augustus John, Derwent Lees and Ian Strang joined him at Arenig on and off over the next two years. His early death from tuberculosis cut short a promising career as an artist.

This watercolour displays the immediacy and intensity of the artist's response to the landscape he discovered at Arenig. The combination of quickly observed drawn features such as the mountain profiles and the tree on the right are all integrated with the watercolour washes used by Innes. The tree defines the scale for the whole picture and has an affinity with the spatial imagery of the Japanese woodblock print. He has used a visual shorthand, for the building on its own hill, and the bird at the bottom, have been reduced to a symbol rather than a description of their form. These early watercolours were later substituted by the many directly observed oil paintings on wood which were painted outside in the landscape.

58. James Dickson Innes, Arenig, *1911, ink and watercolour on paper, 25.4 x 35.6, Tate Britain*

59
James Dickson Innes, *Arenig, North Wales* 1913, oil on plywood panel, 86 x 114, Tate Britain

Arenig, North Wales was the last of a series of paintings of the mountain that Innes first began in 1911. It shows the fast-approaching twilight with the last rays of the setting sun illuminating the mountain's summit peaks in a rosy glow. The technique Innes has used here combines form and image in one all-over application of oil paint to the surface of the board. The paint is used as a drawing tool and gives solidity to the scene without any prior formal drawing. This also contributes to the vivid freshness of these paintings. Innes had seen the Arenig mountain as a motif where colour experimentation could take place. Here he has used a Fauve colour palette and applied it to a desolate and remote piece of Welsh mountain scenery. These inspirational paintings by Innes were a short-lived evocation of his spirit and excitement, captured in paint. A year later he was dead, the First World War had begun and these works were largely forgotten; recently, however, his reputation is being re-assessed and his contribution to British art acknowledged.

59. James Dickson Innes, Arenig, North Wales *1913, oil on plywood panel, 86 x 114, Tate Britain*

60
Augustus Edwin John, *Arenig Mountain*, 1911–12, oil on canvas, 46 x 76, Glynn Vivian Art Gallery, Swansea

Augustus Edwin John (1878–1961) was one of the most gifted draughtsman of the figure in the twentieth century. He was an accomplished society portrait painter and was a highly successful artist during his lifetime. He was born in Tenby and after a brief spell at Tenby Art School attended the Slade School of Fine Art where his gift for drawing was acknowledged by Henry Tonks, one of his tutors. John enjoyed travel both in Britain and in Europe. It was after a visit to the south of France that he joined James Dickson Innes in north Wales to paint the landscape at Arenig. The experience of working alongside Innes on location, using post Impressionist colour and working quickly, was liberating for him. This sojourn lasted from 1911–1912 with some breaks in between to maintain professional commitments. After the First World War John continued working as a portrait artist. He never returned to the spontaneity of the Arenig years and his use of colour became more subdued as the century progressed.

Arenig Mountain by Augustus John is from the viewpoint favoured by Innes and looks directly across to the two summit peaks. This view is painted on canvas and probably pre-dates the paintings John made on wood such as *Llyn Treweryn* with its atmospheric use of bright colour and rapid execution. This work is in Tate Britain. It depicts an expansive view across the moorland lake to distant mountains and is dated 1911–12. This highlights the artistic influence the younger Innes had on John during their Arenig years. For John the experience of working directly in the landscape was not often repeated in future years as he developed his portraits and large scale lyrical compositions.

60. Augustus Edwin John, Arenig Mountain, *1911-12, oil on canvas, 46 x 76, Glynn Vivian Art Gallery, Swansea*

61
Augustus Edwin John, *Llyn Treweryn,* **1911–12, oil on wood, 31.6 x 40.7, Tate Britain**

The influence of James Dickson Innes can be seen in this freely painted oil by Augustus John. The lake is situated close to Arenig Fawr. The view is across the lake towards the distant Rhinog Fawr (720m). John painted this work out of doors, probably in the company of Innes, using high intensity colour. Here John captures the fresh breezy feel of the scene with an economy of means. This was a significant change from John's usual palette of muted hues. It also reflects the impact of post-impressionism on some of the younger British artists.

61. Augustus Edwin John, Llyn Treweryn, *1911-12, oil on wood, 31.6 x 40.7, Tate Britain*

62
Derwent Lees, *Arenig Fawr*, 1911, oil on wood panel, 24.5 x 35, The Potteries Museum and Art Gallery, Stoke on Trent

Derwent Lees (1885–1931) was an Australian landscape artist. He came to England after studying at Melbourne University and spent time in Paris before attending the Slade School of Fine Art from 1905–8. His time at the Slade coincided with the years that Innes was there and the two became close friends. He also knew John and was invited by Innes to join him in north Wales, arriving at Arenig in 1911. Here he painted his views of Arenig and the local area. Lees worked directly from nature using wooden panels and post-impressionist colour. During the period 1908–18 he taught drawing at the Slade and made several visits to Europe, visiting Collioure in 1910. He held a successful one person exhibition at the Chenil Galleries in 1914. From about 1919 onwards he suffered from a serious mental health problem and this led to his premature death in 1931 at the age of forty-six.

Arenig Fawr was painted in 1911 by Derwent Lees on location at Arenig in the company of Innes and John. Here we see the bulk of the mountain filling the picture space. The white areas of winter snow give an abstract quality to the picture and produce a strong tonal contrast throughout the painting. This direct observation gives authenticity to the subject and the improvised painterly technique emphasises this aspect of a direct response to the scene before him. In this composition the mountain form is placed in the centre, with the summit peaks near the top of the painting. The foreground area of lake and foreshore cuts across the whole picture space, almost dividing it, but this awkwardness contributes to the reality of the view. The sky turns from a pale grey to a light wintery blue and highlights the profile of the Arenig mountain.

62. Derwent Lees, Arenig Fawr, *1911, oil on wood panel, 24.5 x 35,*
The Potteries Museum and Art Gallery, Stoke on Trent

63
Clyde Holmes, *Billowing Cloud, Snowdonia*, 1987, oil on board, 80 x 102, National Library of Wales

Clyde Holmes (1940–2008) was a landscape painter and eco-poet. He was born in London and after leaving school worked as a session musician before going to Hornsey College of Art. He then studied fine art at St Martins School of Art from 1965 to 1968. After working at the British Library he decided to leave London for a Welsh farmhouse in Cwm Hesgin, a remote location in southern Snowdonia, so he could be close to his chosen subject matter in both painting and poetry. This was the wild mountain landscape close to where he lived. The mountain views are seen through various weather conditions that form part of the landscape around the Arenigs. His published poetry includes *Skywalls – A Snowdonia Sequence*, published in 1998 and *Featherpaths*, published in 2004. In 1997 he was featured in the BBC 2 'Visions of Snowdonia' series narrated by Sir Anthony Hopkins. In 2005 he undertook a project that compared the lakes of Finland with those of north Wales. and these works were shown in the exhibition 'Watermarks' in 2007. His work is in both private and public collections in the UK and abroad.

The painting, *Billowing Cloud, Snowdonia* dates from 1987 and shows an archetypal landscape of mountain and cloud. The composition is reminiscent of Samuel Palmer's (1805–1881) painting of 1834, T*he White Cloud* which is in the Ashmolean Museum, Oxford. In Holmes' picture the right-hand foreground area is painted in a range of orange and browns. The contrasting dark area in the middle distance and the horizon profile contrast with the lighter and more ethereal treatment of the cloud itself. Holmes is concerned with nature and the effects of the weather on the landscape and how it is perceived. In this oil painting the artist has achieved a directness of approach that reveals a type of mountain landscape that is often overlooked in favour of a more recognisable location. The artist often painted elevated mountain vistas close to his house and studio rather than depicting well-known mountain subjects. The lack of an identifiable location in the title of this work emphasises the apparent ordinariness of the view chosen by Holmes, compelling the viewer to focus on the contrast between light and shadow rather than the topography.

63. *Clyde Holmes,* Billowing Cloud, Snowdonia, *1987, oil on board, 80 x 102, National Library of Wales*

NINE
Betws-y-coed and its Mountain Scenery

Betws-y-coed was a stopping-off place on Thomas Telford's coach road through north Wales. The Royal Oak Hotel became a favoured place to stay on this route through the heart of Snowdonia. David Cox (1783–1859) stayed there most summers between 1844 and 1856 and used it as a base to explore the surrounding mountain scenery. It has been recorded that Cox would lay his watercolours out on his bed to dry. The nearby Pont-y-Pair bridge over the Llugwy was a landmark that was dramatically illustrated by Paul Sandby (1730–1809) in his first set of aquatint prints, published in 1776. His aquatint shows the river in full flood and the view upstream is much more open than it is today due to the increased tree growth in the valley. This viewpoint towards the bridge, and from the bridge looking upstream, has been repeated and replicated many times since Sandby's early image was made.

Cox himself attracted both patrons and artists to the village and passed on his knowledge of the best locations for landscape scenery available nearby. This legacy continued after his death in 1859 and artists continued to be attracted to this spot made more accessible by the arrival of the railway in 1868. The Royal Oak had already been enlarged by 1861 to meet the increased demand. From this period a number of artists made their homes in the village and in the nearby Conwy valley. Clarence Whaite (1828–1912) lived here from 1870, having been a frequent visitor since meeting David Cox in 1852. The outbreak of the First World War marked the end of this flourishing artistic colony.

Thomas Pennant observations on Betws-y-coed, from *A Tour in Wales*:

A little farther, pass by Pont y Pair, a most singular bridge, flung over the Llugwy, consisting of five arches, placed on the rude rocks, which form most durable piers. These rocks are precipitous, and in high floods exhibit to the passenger most awful cataracts below the bridge. The scenery beyond, of rocky mountains, fringed with woods, is very striking.

Thomas Pennant, *A Tour in Wales*, vol. 2., London, 1784, p.144.

Detail of Plate 64. David Cox, The river Llugwy above Betws-y-Coed North Wales

Plates 64-69

64
David Cox, *The river Llugwy above Betws-y-Coed North Wales*, 1845, watercolour, 21 x 28, private collection

David Cox (1783–1859) was a Birmingham based artist whose earliest watercolours of Wales date from his first visit in 1805. From 1844 to 1856 he spent the summer months at Betws-y-coed, either at the Royal Oak Hotel or at a nearby cottage in the village. From here he was able to make sketching trips into the heart of Snowdonia's mountains and paint its scenery. Many of these subjects were reworked for the London exhibitions. A number of watercolour sketches made on location were exhibited in the various watercolour societies. Cox was often able to sell his drawings and sketches of mountain scenery directly to an ever increasing audience of admirers as his reputation grew. This following included other artists seeking mountain scenery who were also making Betws-y-coed their preferred base.

The river Llugwy above Betws-y-Coed shows the view upstream from a point just beyond the Pont-y-Pair bridge. The 'Cauldron Bridge' was a favourite spot to witness the spectacular rush of water caused by some large boulders in the stream bed. This area was only a short walk from the centre of the village and the Royal Oak Hotel. This watercolour shows the view upstream with the carefully observed hanging rock above the river on the right, through to the distant Craig Wen. In this work Cox demonstrates his ability to capture the whole scene, using a painterly technique with no one part given more status than another. Here Cox juxtaposes the complementary colours of blue and orange to great effect. His use of descriptive colour contributes to the painting's realism such as in his treatment of running water. His choice of subject, trees, river, rock, mountain, sky, is very characteristic of his Betws-y-coed watercolours.

64. *David Cox,* The river Llugwy above Betws-y-Coed North Wales, *1845, watercolour, 21 x 28, private collection*

65
Frederick Henry Henshaw, *Dinas Betws-y-Coed, North Wales*, 1851, oil on canvas, 71 x 91.5, Government Art Collection

Frederick Henry Henshaw (1807–1891) was part of a group of artists now known as the Birmingham School, a group of landscape painters. He worked in both watercolour and in oil, and painted landscapes in all areas of England, Wales and Scotland. He also travelled to Italy and painted watercolours in Rome. He exhibited widely, including the Royal Birmingham Society of Artists and at the Royal Academy in London. He lived in the Small Heath area of Birmingham and witnessed the increasing loss of countryside as Birmingham expanded. This aspect of change in rural life he recorded in his watercolours and they now provide a visual record of a lost rural landscape.

Dinas Betws-y-Coed depicts a view just outside the village and shows the steep rugged mountain terrain that was within easy reach, yet appears remote. It is almost certain that Henshaw knew Cox and took advice on potential subjects. This oil painting dates from the period that Cox stayed in Betws-y-coed. There is a similar view by Cox in the Birmingham Museum and Art Gallery dated 1846. In Henshaw's painting the composition is carefully constructed, yet understated, with the emphasis on the rock strata which has been carefully recorded and reflects the new interests in geology at this time. The colour is naturalistic and adds to the realism of the picture. The lack of any foreground area at the bottom edge of the image hints at the sublime, yet the overall effect is picturesque.

65. *Frederick Henry Henshaw,* Dinas Betws-y-Coed, North Wales, *1851, oil on canvas, 71 x 91.5, Government Art Collection*

66
Alfred William Hunt, *Dolwyddelan Castle North Wales*, 1856, watercolour on paper, 27.4 x 38.4, British Museum, London

Alfred William Hunt (1830–1896) was born in Liverpool. He studied Classics at Corpus Christi College, Oxford and in 1851 he won the Newdigate Prize for Poetry. After this he resumed his interest in art and started to practise landscape painting in both watercolour and oil. Ruskin suggested he exhibit at the Royal Academy, which he did from 1854 onwards. He also exhibited at the many watercolour societies in London. In 1862, the year after his marriage, he was elected to the Old Watercolour Society, becoming a full member in 1864. He took up many of Ruskin's ideas and he was also influenced by the work of J. M. W. Turner and by the Pre-Raphaelite Brotherhood, particularly in their ability to paint minutely observed detail from nature. Hunt was able to absorb these various influences and make them his own, producing a unique approach to landscape painting. The atmospheric effects he sought, he found in the mountains of Snowdonia, the Lake District and in the Alps. His work is represented in many public collections such as the British Museum, Tate Britain and the V&A, and in private collections.

In this expansive watercolour of the Dolwyddelan valley, Hunt has shown the thirteenth-century castle in the middle distance on the right side of the picture. The castle has been placed carefully on the golden section within the composition. The square castle is dwarfed by the surrounding mountains that close in the vale towards Betws-y-coed. In the foreground can be seen the river Lledr and sheep grazing. The minutely applied brush strokes and the use of complementary colour in a sequence of blue and orange give the picture a prismatic quality unique to the artist. Hunt visited this location in 1856 on his second visit to north Wales in search of dramatic mountain scenery. However, on this visit the weather was often too bad to work outside. Hunt returned to north Wales in 1857 and painted a dramatic watercolour titled *Mount Snowdon Through Clearing Clouds* (private collection) that evokes a sense of awe in front of untamed nature.

66. *Alfred William Hunt,* Dolwyddelan Castle North Wales, *1856, watercolour on paper, 27.4 x 38.4, British Museum, London*

67
Henry Clarence Whaite, *The Rainbow*, 1862, oil on canvas, 139.7 x 241.6, Nottingham City Museums and Galleries, (Castle Museum)

Henry Clarence Whaite (1828–1912) was a Manchester based landscape painter who studied at the Manchester School of Design. He then attended classes at the Royal Academy in London. He travelled abroad and became aware of mountain scenery in Switzerland; upon his return he sought out the mountain scenery available in Britain. The north Wales landscape was to provide Whaite with all he required for his art to flourish a little closer to Manchester than the Alps! The small village of Betws-y-coed, lying close to the main mountains of Snowdonia, gave Whaite a base from which to explore his subject, as David Cox had done earlier. A number of artists chose to move to the village in the second half of the nineteenth century and began to establish a loose knit group. This association of artists has recently been referred to as the Betws-y-coed Artist Colony.

Whaite later moved to the Conwy Valley and, unlike Cox, was able to paint the mountains throughout the year; many of his landscape views show snow on the higher Welsh mountains. As discussed earlier (chapter Three), Whaite had seen Frederick Edwin Church's famous large painting, *The Heart of the Andes* in London in 1859; a work which made a significant impact on Whaite and certainly encouraged him to make large scale oil paintings of Welsh mountain scenery.

The Rainbow was exhibited at the Royal Academy in 1862. It is a very large work which was begun in 1861, originally based on numerous studies from nature. Later, the actual canvas was partly painted on location in a temporary outdoor studio. The location Whaite has used is high on the foothills between Betws-y-coed and Capel Curig. The season represented is spring, with the highest mountains in the distance covered with snow. The vista is partly obscured and a magnificent rainbow is visible on the left, disappearing into the vaporous mist at the centre of the picture. The influence of Church's 1859 painting *The Heart of the Andes* can be seen, particularly in the microscopic brush work and detailed prismatic colouration. Another similar feature is the left-to-right compositional structure Whaite has used. Like Church's picture the inclusion of figures in the immediate foreground adds to the scale and grandeur of the overall scene. Another oil painting by

Whaite, titled, *A Welsh Funeral (To the Cold Earth)* of 1865, depicts a scene near Betws-y-coed with a distant panorama of Snowdonia's mountains behind the mourners. It is also in the Nottingham Castle Museum.

> Review of The Rainbow from Manchester Guardian, September 1862
>
> *The texture of the cloud is perfect; the forest of trunks and branches is truth itself; and nothing can exceed the beauty of the half clothed rocks on the left, with the patches of young grass creeping over them. The picture as a whole is a finished poem of pastoral beauty.*
>
> Peter Lord, *The Betws-y-coed Artists' Colony 1844-1914*, National Library of Wales, 1998, p.99

67. Henry Clarence Whaite, The Rainbow, *1862, oil on canvas, 139.7 x 241.6, Nottingham City Museums and Galleries, (Castle Museum)*

68
Benjamin Williams Leader, *Betws-y-Coed*, c.1865, oil on mill board, 16.2 x 23.2, Victoria and Albert Museum, London

Benjamin Williams Leader (1831–1923) was a professional landscape painter in oils. He was brought up in Worcester and attended the Worcester School of Design. He studied at the Royal Academy Schools from 1854 although he did not finish his studies there. His landscape subjects include pastoral scenes in Worcestershire and the Severn valley and mountain landscapes in Scotland and Wales. The artist and his family moved to Shere, Surrey in 1889 and this remained his base until his death in 1923.

Betws-y-Coed is a small oil painting and was probably started outside. It is reminiscent of the small plein air works of David Cox, with a seemingly unplanned composition that makes no pretence to grandeur. The composition does adhere to the general principles of the golden section with the right-hand mountain dividing the picture in an attractive way, leading the eye from the right through to the distant horizon on the left. The technique here is more naturalistic than the previous, more Pre-Raphaelite and detailed style he had used. The brownish and golden colouring suggest a late evening light at the end of the summer, or a scene in early autumn. In the centre foreground can be seen two travelling figures with horses and baskets. Leader often made small preliminary oil studies before beginning a larger work and this may well be one of these.

68. **Benjamin Williams Leader,** Betws-y-Coed, *c.1865, oil on mill board, 16.2 x 23.2, Victoria and Albert Museum, London*

69
Roland Vivian Pitchforth, *Snowdonia*, c.1954, watercolour, 47 x 62.5, private collection

Roland Vivian Pitchforth (1895–1982) was primarily a landscape painter, although he also produced some fine portraits and was an official war artist during the Second World War. Born in Yorkshire, he attended Wakefield and Leeds Schools of Art from 1912 to 1915. He returned to Leeds after war service to complete his course 1919–1921 and won a scholarship to study at the Royal College of Art from 1922 to 1925. He worked in both oil and watercolour, but from 1945 onwards almost entirely in watercolour. This was at a time when watercolour was out of favour and Pitchforth did much to invigorate the medium. His preferred subject matter was the coastal scenery around the south of England but he also painted in Scotland and in north Wales. He taught at several London Art Schools both before and after the Second World War. He was a highly regarded teacher, particularly in the life room. Pitchforth first exhibited at the Royal Academy in 1941 and was elected ARA in 1942 and RA in 1953. During his career he exhibited at many London galleries both private and public. Examples of his work can be found in many national collections including Tate Britain and the Victoria & Albert Museum.

Snowdonia is a large and expansive watercolour that presents a distant view towards the highest mountains of Snowdonia. This panoramic view of mountains is very similar to the vista that can be seen from the upland area to the east of Betws-y-coed. Pitchforth visited this area of north Wales more than once, staying at Porthmadog and at nearby Conwy. This watercolour was painted outside on the spot as the many clamp marks on the edge of the paper testify. The feeling of a vast space is heightened by the beautiful and delicate colour scheme the artist has applied. The light sky with its subtle use of pink sits above the silhouetted pale tones of the main mountain forms at centre left. The dissolving horizon adds to the sense of depth in the painting. The technique of blending colour washes into others gives an immediacy to the scene. The whole effect is a complete visual experience of place captured in a single sitting. On occasions in north Wales, Pitchforth would make small sketchbook drawings in the landscape adding colour notes for later use. These watercolours were painted indoors, unlike the work seen here.

Roland Vivian Pitchforth, Snowdonia, *c.1954, watercolour, 47 x 62.5 private collection*

Endnotes

[1] Thomas Roscoe, *Wanderings and Excursions in North Wales*, London, 1836 p. 128.
[2] Thomas Pennant, *A Tour in Wales*, vol 2, London, 1784, p.159.
[3] Thomas Pennant, *A Tour in Wales*, 2 vols., London, p 189.
[4] Rev. G. J. Freeman, *Sketches in Wales, or a Diary of Three Walking Excursions in that Principality in the Years 1823, 1824, 1825*, London, 1826, p. 216.
[5] Paul Joyner, Cader Idris, exhibition catalogue, National Library of Wales, 2001.
[6] J. M. W. Turner, *Pont Aberglaslyn, Welsh Mountains and a River*, c.1799, 33 x 22.8, graphite and watercolour, in Lancashire and North Wales Sketchbook, no. XLV, Turner Bequest, Tate Britain, reference no. D01920.
[7] Thomas Pennant, *A Tour in Wales*, London, 1784. vol. 2, p. 163.
[8] E. Pugh, Cambria Depicta, London, 1816 pp.111–12.
[9] John Ruskin, Modern Painters, vol. 4, Of Mountain Beauty, (1856), London, 1910, p. 178.

Further Reading

Malcolm Andrews, *In Search for the Picturesque: Landscape Aesthetics and Tourism in Britain, 1760-1800*, Scolar Press, Aldershot, 1990.

John Barrell, *Edward Pugh of Ruthin 1763-1813: "A Native Artist"*. Gwasg Prifysgol Cymru - University of Wales Press, Cardiff. 2013.

Peter Bicknell, *British Hills and Mountains*, Collins, London, 1947.

David Kirk, *Snowdonia: A Historical Anthology*, Gwasg Carreg Gwalch, Llanrwst, 1994.

Peter Lord, *Clarence Whaite and the Welsh Art World: The Betws-y-coed Artists' Colony, 1844-1914*, National Library of Wales, Aberystwyth,1998.

Thomas Pennant, *A Tour in Wales*, 2 vols., London, 1784, reprint editions available.

Artists' websites:
The majority of late twentieth century artists and contemporary artists featured in this book have their own websites. Search on-line using their name followed by the word artist.

Art Collections
The National Library of Wales and the National Museum of Wales have a large collection of pictures and related material. The Royal Cambrian Academy in Conwy and MOMA Wales in Machynlleth regularly hold exhibitions of contemporary Welsh landscape painting. There are substantial holdings of pictures in many British institutions particularly in Tate Britain and at the British Museum.

Index of Artist Entries

William Henry Barnard 112
Thomas Mann Baynes 56
Edmund Becker 28
Peter Bishop 104
David Cox 96, 116, 128, 166
Thomas Creswick 30
Joshua Cristall 58, 80
Tom Cross 100
Pete Davis 102
Myles Birket Foster 118
Russell Gilder 122
Samuel H Grimm 22, 108
Moses Griffith 24, 36, 110
Frederick Henry Henshaw 168
Clyde Holmes 162
Kevan Hopson 82
Herbert Edwin Pelham Hughes-Stanton 98
Alfred William Hunt 134, 170
James Dickson Innes 152, 154
Samuel Jackson 94, 130
Augustus John 156, 158
Benjamin Williams Leader 120, 176
Derwent Lees 160
Charles William Mansel Lewis 136
Phillippe Jacques de Loutherbourg 34
Robert A Newell 68
Francis Nicholson 114
Sidney Richard Percy 60
John Piper 140
Roland Vivian Pitchforth 178
Edward Pugh 42, 132
Peter Prendergast 146
George Fennel Robson 126
Paul Sandby 20, 72
John Warwick Smith 52
George Grainger Smith 44
John James Stewart 76
David Tress 66
Thomas Tudor 78, 90
Joseph Mallord William Turner 26, 38, 54
Cornelius Varley 74
John Varley 40
James Ward 92

Henry Clarence Whaite 62, 172
Kyffin Williams 64, 142
Richard Wilson 48, 88
Matthew Wood 84
David Woodford 148

Glossary of Terms

Aesthetics
The appreciation of beauty. A set of principles that underpin artistic practice and issues of taste.

Alla Prima
Art work made in a single session, often outside.

Aquatint
A printmaking process that imitates the broad flat tonal washes of watercolour. A copper plate is covered with powdered resin and is etched by acid using a combination of etching tools. A printing press is used to transfer the ink from the plate to the heavy absorbent print paper.

British Institution
The British Institution was a private gallery founded in 1805. It was located at 52 Pall Mall, London from 1806 until 1867. It held exhibitions of art from the past and also showed the work of contemporary artists in temporary exhibitions where works were for sale.

Chiaroscuro
Contrast of light and dark in a picture.

Classical
A set of ideal forms that have their origins in both Greek and Roman antiquity. A concept of ideal beauty as seen in the landscape paintings of Claude and Poussin. In the UK the formal landscaped gardens of many country house estates are modelled on classical lines, characterised by their artificial lakes, temples and open vistas framed by trees.

Complementary Colour
Pairs of colours that lie directly opposite each other on the colour circle. Used in juxtaposition they set up a strong vibration between the two. These are primary red and secondary green; blue and orange; yellow and purple.

Engraving
A linear printmaking process where a copper metal plate is incised with a burin. The plate is inked and printed under pressure. The ink is forced out of the cut grooves and sits raised up on the paper surface.

Etching
An intaglio printmaking process that relies on a ground. A layer of wax is applied to the metal plate and the image is scratched on to the surface. It is then placed in an acid bath to etch the plate ready for printing. The acid bites in to the plate producing the grooves to take the ink. Face up in the press the whole plate is inked and then wiped away with only the remaining ink left to print. It is then printed on to dampened paper under pressure.

Fauvism
Fauve paintings are characterised by the use of strong vibrant colour applied directly to the canvas with no attempt at naturalism. The French movement lasted from 1905 to 1907. Matisse and Derain produced the best examples of the new style.

Grosvenor Gallery
The Grosvenor Gallery was founded in Bond Street in 1877. It showcased a range of contemporary art especially artists from the aesthetic movement. It closed in 1890.

Golden Section or Golden Mean
A term used to describe an aesthetically pleasing set of proportions within a picture. It is roughly a ratio of three to five. Most windows have this proportion and this composition formula is common in landscape painting such as in John Constable's large oil paintings.

Impasto
An art term that applies to a layer of paint laid thickly on to a canvas or board. An Impasto surface is usually highly textured and uneven and it can have a three-dimensional appearance.

Intaglio
Refers to various printmaking processes where the image is cut or sunken so it will retain ink. It is the opposite of a relief print where the area to be printed is raised rather than incised. Examples include etching and line engraving.

Lithography
A printmaking process that uses a flat stone or metal plate which goes through a chemical process only allowing the drawn areas to accept ink and be printed. By using a large off-set press images can be printed on large sheets of paper. Chromolithography was an ideal method for the reproduction of posters in colour with each colour requiring a separate stone and printing.

Local Colour
The appearance of natural colour in painting. True colours in nature not changed by external influences such as a shadow or reflective light.

Old Watercolour Society (OWS)
See "Society of Painters in Watercolour"

Plein Air
Plein air is a French term. It describes any painting made outside in the open air. It can also refer to a particular quality of daylight only experienced outside.

Picturesque
The term was established by William Gilpin in 1768 in his published essay on prints to highlight that aspect of beauty which is pleasing in a picture. Its characteristic tripartite compositional structure became a valuable shorthand for many artists making a "picturesque tour".

Picturesque Tour
The picturesque tour was established by Gilpin's tour down the River Wye, which he wrote about and published in 1782. It was illustrated in aquatints highlighting the most pleasing aspects of nature, and informed visitors where the best views were. Later picturesque tours were made in other locations such as in the Lake District and north Wales

Pre Raphaelites – Pre-Raphaelite Brotherhood
Formed initially by a small group of artists and writers in 1848. The aim of the group was to paint in clear bright colours as artists had before the time of Raphael. The style became established by 1850. An example is Ophelia (1850-1851) by John Everett Millais, shown at the Royal Academy. Other artists who were not original members also chose to paint in the "truth to nature" style until the end of the 19th century.

Prismatic Colour
Prismatic colour refers to the whole range of bright colours as seen through a prism or in a rainbow. In painting these colours are used directly without any pre-mixing. Characteristically these paintings are bright and include all the colours of the spectrum.

Romantic Movement
The heyday of this movement in art was from 1800 to about 1840. In landscape painting it was more of an emotional response to the power of nature over the literal. Feeling and passion took precedence and mountain scenery was particularly favoured for this treatment.

Royal Academy of Arts
The Royal Academy of Arts was founded in December 1768 by King George III and a group of 34 founder members as an artist-run independent organisation. It was an exhibition venue and it also provided free education for artists in the RA Schools.

The first President was Joshua Reynolds. It had many homes but in 1868 it moved to Burlington House, Piccadilly, London. The annual Summer Show has been held every year since 1769 without interruption and this is a unique record. Members are elected representing many artistic disciplines including architecture. The Royal Academy is entirely self supporting financially.

Royal Cambrian Academy
The Royal Cambrian Academy was originally founded in north Wales in 1881 by a group of mostly English landscape painters, many of whom were resident in or around Betws-y-coed and the Conwy valley, or who visited the location from the Manchester area. In 1996 a purpose-built gallery space was opened adjacent to the original Plas Mawr building in Conwy. The aim of the Academy is to promote excellence in Welsh contemporary art.

Society of British Artists
Established in London in 1823. The original membership consisted of 23 and the first exhibitions took place in 1824. It became known as the Royal Society of British Artists in 1887. Originally located in Suffolk Street, today the RBA holds exhibitions in the Mall Galleries as part of the Federation of British Artists and has 112 members.

Society of Painters in Watercolour
(sometimes referred to as the Old Watercolour Society) Founded in 1804 to promote watercolour painting, which at the time the members felt was not receiving enough exposure on the walls of the Royal Academy. Between 1812 and 1820 the society included oil painting. From 1820 onwards it reverted to its original title and was once again exclusively a watercolour society. In 1881 the society obtained its royal status. In 1988 the present name was established as the Royal Watercolour Society, often abbreviated to RWS.

Sublime
Edmund Burke's "A Philosophical Enquiry into the Origin of Our Ideas of the Sublime and Beautiful", first published in 1757 laid out his definitions of the sublime. The categories of darkness, grandeur, obscurity, vastness, loftiness and awe were all associated with Burke. Sublime subjects include the sea, mountains, chasms, gorges and effects of nature such as storms, lightning strikes, etc., all have the capacity for a 'sublime' treatment by artists.

Tonal
A gradation of light to dark or dark to light in painting, drawing or print.

Topographical
The detailed representation of place or architectural subject made in a range of visual media. Visual accuracy was the prime ingredient of topographical art rather than artistic emotion or self expression. It was often used as the basis for print reproduction particularly for engraving in the 18th century and lithography in the 19th.

Tripartite Composition
A picture divided into three parts or planes. A compositional structure favoured by William Gilpin the instigator of the picturesque.

Watercolour
A fluid paint medium consisting of a range of coloured pigments held together in a binding medium usually gum arabic. It becomes water soluble when water is added to the individual pans of colour. The colour is then applied to the support, usually a heavyweight paper.

Select Bibliography

Alison, Archibald, *Essays on the Nature and Principals of Taste*, (1790) Edinburgh, 1825.

Andrews, Malcolm, *The Search for the Picturesque: Landscape Aesthetics and Tourism in Britain, 1760–1800*, Scolar Press, Aldershot, 1989.

Barber, Carl, *William Gilpin, His Drawings, Teaching and the Theory of the Picturesque*, Oxford, 1963.

Barrell, John, *The Dark Side of the Landscape: The Rural Poor in English Painting 1730–1840*, Cambridge University Press, Cambridge, 1980.

Barrell, John, *Edward Pugh of Ruthin 1763–1813: A Native Artist, (Wales and the French Revolution)*, University of Wales Press, Aberystwyth, 2013.

Bell, David, *The Artist in Wales,* George G Harrap & Co. London, 1957.

Bermingham, Ann, *Landscape and Ideology: The English Rustic Tradition 1740–1860,* University of California Press, Berkley, 1986.

Bicknell, Peter, *British Hills and Mountains,* Collins, London, 1947.

Bingley, William, *North Wales Delineated from Two Excursions through all the Interesting Parts of that Highly Interesting and Romantic Country, and Intended as a Guide to Future Tourists,* Longman, Hurst, Rees, Orme and Brown, London, 1814.

Bishop, Peter, 'Rich and Varied Prospects: Mountain Scenery in Snowdonia 1764–1836: Thomas Pennant's 'A Tour in Wales' and its Influence,* MA thesis, University of Central England in Birmingham, 1995.

Bishop, Peter, *Vision and Revision: Mountain Scenery in Snowdonia, 1750–1880*, PhD thesis, Vol. 1– Text, Vol. 2 – Illustrations, Aberystwyth University, 2001.

Bishop, Peter, 'Cader Idris Wilson's View' in *Peter Bishop, Cader Idris*, exhibition catalogue, Peter Bishop & Museum of Modern Art Wales, 2012. pp. 12-20.

Bogle, James, *Artists in Snowdonia,* Y Lolfa Cyf., Talybont, 1990.

Brennan, Matthew, *Wordsworth, Turner, and Romantic Landscape: A Study of the .Traditions of the Picturesque and the Sublime,* Columbia State College & Camden House, London, 1987.

Cradock, Joseph, *An Account of some of the most Romantic Parts of North Wales,* T. Davies and T. Cadell, London, 1777.

Daniels, Stephen, *Fields of Vision: Landscape Imagery and National Identity In England and the United States,* Polity Press, Cambridge, 1994.

Daniels, Stephen, & Watkins, Charles, eds., *The Picturesque Landscape: Visions of Georgian Herefordshire*, exhibition catalogue, Department of Geography, University of Nottingham & Hereford City Art Gallery, Nottingham, 1994.

Davis, Pete, 'Richard Wilson and Cader Idris', in *Cader Idris Soul of a Lonely Place*, exhibition catalogue, University of Wales Press, Aberystwyth, 1997, no pagination.

Davis, Pete, 'Mountains and Memory'. In *Peter Bishop Cader Idris*, exhibition catalogue, Peter Bishop and Museum of Modern Art Wales, pp. 6–11.

Drabble, Margaret, 'The Future of our Past', in *Towards a new landscape,* Bernard Jacobson Limited, 1993, pp. 33-38.

Evans, J., *The Beauties of England and Wales: or Delineations Topographical, Illustrated and Descriptive – North Wales,* J. Harris, Venor etc., London, 1812.

Evans, Ronald Paul, *Thomas Pennant's writings on North Wales*, MA thesis, University of Wales, Swansea, 1985.

Evans, Ronald Paul, *The life and work of Thomas Pennant (1726–1798)*, PhD thesis, University of Wales, Swansea, 1994.

Ford, Brinsley, 'Sir Watkin Williams Wynn, A Welsh Maecenas', Apollo, June 1974, pp. 435-439.

Fraser-Jenkins, A. D., 'The Romantic Traveller in Wales', Bulletin of the National Museum of Wales, Cardiff, Winter, 1970, pp. 28-37.

Fraser-Jenkins, A. D., *J. D. Innes at the National Museum of Wales*, reference catalogue, National Museum of Wales, Cardiff, 1975.

Fraser-Jenkins, David, & Munro, Melissa, *John Piper: The Mountains of Wales*, exhibition catalogue, National Museum of Wales, Cardiff, 2012.

Freeman, G. J., *Sketches in Wales, or a Diary of Three Walking Excursions in that Principality in the Years 1823, 1824, 1825*, Longman, Rees, Orme, Brown and Green, London, 1826.

Gage, John, 'Turner and the Picturesque', Burlington Magazine, pp. 16-22, part two, pp. 75-80.

Gilpin, William, *Three Essays: On Picturesque Beauty; on Picturesque Travel; and on Sketching Landscape: to which is added a Poem on Landscape Painting,* (1792) T. Cadell & W. Davies, Strand, London, 1808.

Gilpin, William, *Observations on the River Wye, and Several Parts of South Wales, Relative chiefly to Picturesque Beauty; made in the Summer of the Year 1770,* (1783) R Blamire, Strand, London, 1789.

Grigson, Geoffrey, *Britain Observed: The Landscape through artists eyes*, Phaidon Press, London, 1975.

Hackforth-Jones, Jocelyn, *Views in Wales c. 1760–1830*, PhD thesis, University of Sydney, 1988.

Hawes, Louis, *Presences of Nature: British Landscape, 1780–1830*, exhibition catalogue, Yale Center for British Art, New Haven & London, 1982.

Hayes, John, 'British Patrons and landscape: The response to nature in the eighteenth century', Apollo, June 1966, pp. 441-451.

Herrmann, Luke, British Landscape Painting of the Eighteenth Century, Faber & Faber, London, 1973.

Herrmann, Luke, Paul and Thomas Sandby, B. T. Batsford & Victoria & Albert Museum, London, 1986.

Hipple, W., The Beautiful, the Sublime, and the Picturesque in Eighteenth Century British Aesthetic Theory, Carbondale, 1957.

Howard, Peter, Changing Taste in Landscape Art, PhD thesis, University of Exeter, 1984.

Howard, Peter, Landscapes: the Artists Vision, Routledge, London, 1991.

Hughes, Peter, Paul Sandby and Sir Watkin Williams-Wynn, Burlington Magazine, CXIV, 1972, pp. 459- 466.

Hunt, John Dixon, 'Picturesque Mirrors and the Ruins of the Past', Art History 4, No. 2, September, 1981.

Hussey, Christopher, The Picturesque: Studies in a Point of View, Frank Cass & Co. Ltd., London, 1927.

Ingles, Fred, 'Landscape as popular culture', Landscape Research, Vol. 12., no. 3, 1987, pp. 20-25.

Jacobs, Michael, & Warner, Malcolm, Art in Wales, Phaidon Press, Oxford, 1980.

Jeffrey, Ian, 'Public Problems and Private Experience in British Art and Literature', in Judy Collins & Nicola Bennett eds., Landscape in Britain 1850- 1950, exhibition catalogue, Arts Council of Great Britain, London, 1983.

James, Stephanie, Charles Mansel Lewis: Painter, Patron and Promotor of Art in Wales, University of Wales Centre for Advanced Welsh and Celtic Studies, Aberystwyth, 1998.

Joyner, Paul, A Place for a Poussin: a study of Art and artists in Wales, c. 1750- 1850 with a handlist of artists working in Wales c. 1750–1850, 2 vols., PhD thesis, University of Cambridge, 1988.

Joyner, Paul, ed., Dolbadarn, Studies on a Theme, exhibition catalogue, National Library of Wales, Aberystwyth, 1990.

Joyner, Paul, Thomas Tudor 1785–1855: An Artist from Monmouth, exhibition catalogue, National Library of Wales, 1996.

Joyner, Paul, Artists in Wales c.1740-c.1851: A handlist of artists living and working in Wales from c. 1740 up to c. 1851, National Library of Wales, Aberystwyth, 1997.

Joyner, Paul, Afon Conwy, exhibition catalogue, National Library of Wales, 1997.

Kauffmann, C. M., John Varley 1778–1842, B. T. Batsford & Victoria & Albert Museum, London, 1984.

Klonk, Charlotte, Science and the Perception of Nature; British Landscape Art in the Late Eighteenth and Early Nineteenth Centuries, Yale University Press, New Haven & London, 1996.

(PhD thesis, University of Cambridge, 1992).

Kirk, David, Snowdonia, a historical anthology, Gwsag Carreg Gwalch Press, Llanrwst, 1994.

Knight, Richard Payne, An Analytical Enquiry into the Principals of Taste, (1805) London, 1808.

Libson, Lowell, Breadth and Quality: Oil studies, Watercolours and Drawings by James Ward RA, exhibition catalogue, Lowell Libson Ltd., London, 2013.

Lord, Peter, Clarence Whaite and the Welsh Art World: The Betws-y-coed Artists' Colony 1844–1914, National Library of Wales, Aberystwyth, 1998.

Lord, Peter, The Visual Culture of Wales: Imaging the Nation, University of Wales Press, Cardiff, 2000.

Mainwaring, Elizabeth, Italian Landscape in Eighteenth Century England: A Study Chiefly of the Influence of Claude Lorrain and Salvator on English Taste, 1700–1800, (1925) Frank Cass & Co. Ltd., London, 1965.

Marsh, Terry, The Summits of Snowdonia: A guide to the 600-metre summits of Snowdonia, Robert Hale Ltd., London, 1984.

Martin, A., Content and Culture in Victorian Painting: attitudes to Landscape, M.Phil. Thesis, University College London, 1988

Mc Carthy, Francis, The treatment of mountain scenery by some British writers and artists in the eighteenth century – with some special attention to North Wales, 2 vols., PhD thesis, University of Cambridge, 1963.

Moir, Esther, The Discovery of Britain: The English Tourist, 1540–1840, Routledge & Kegan Paul, London, 1964.

Moore, Donald, ed., Wales in the Eighteenth Century, Christopher Davies, Swansea, 1976.

Moore, Donald, Moses Griffith: Artist and Illustrator in the service of Thomas Pennant, exhibition catalogue, Welsh Arts Council, Cardiff, 1979.

Munro, Jane, British Landscape Watercolours 1750–1850, exhibition catalogue, Herbert Press & Fitzwilliam Museum, Cambridge, 1994.

Newell, Christopher, The Grosvenor Gallery Exhibition: Change and Continuity in the Victorian art world, Cambridge University Press, Cambridge, 1995.

Newell, Christopher, The Poetry of Truth; Alfred William Hunt and the Art of Landscape, exhibition catalogue, Ashmolean Museum, Oxford, 2006.

Newell, Robert Hasell, Letters on the Scenery of Wales, including a series of subjects for the pencil, with their stations. Determined on a General Principal: and Instructions to Pedestrian Tourists, Baldwin Craddoock & Joy, London, 1821.

Nicholson, Kathleen, 'Naturalizing Time / Temporalizing Nature:

Turner's Transformation of Landscape Painting', in Katherine Baetjer, ed., *Glorious Nature: British Landscape Painting, 1750–1850*, Hudson Hills Press & A Zwemmer Ltd., London, 1993, pp. 31-46.

Nicholson, Marjorie, *Mountain Gloom and Mountain Glory: The Development of the Aesthetics of the Infinite*, Cornell University Press, New York, 1959.

Nygren, Edward, *James Ward's Gordale Scar: An Essay in the Sublime*, exhibition catalogue, Tate Gallery Publications, London, 1982.

Pennant, Thomas, *A Tour in Wales*, 2 vols., Benjamin White at Horace's Head, London, 1784.

Piglet, Michael, 'Cornelius Varley, Cotman, and the Graphic Telescope', Burlington Magazine, CXIV, 1972, pp. 781-786.

Poucher, Walter, *The Welsh Peaks: A Pictorial Guide to walking in this region and to the safe ascent of its principal mountain groups*, (1962) Constable & Company Ltd., London, 1987.

Price, Uvedale, *An Essay on the Picturesque as compared with the Sublime and the Beautiful*, vol. 2., London, 1798.

Pugh, Edward, *Cambria Depicta: A Tour Through North Wales, illustrated with Picturesque View. By a Native Artist*, W. Charles, London, 1816.

Robertson, Bruce, *The Art of Paul Sandby*, exhibition catalogue, Yale Center for British Art, New Haven, 1985.

Roberts, Askew, *the Gossiping Guide to Wales: Pictorial Itinerary and Snowdon Panorama*, (1869) Hodder & Stoughton, London, 1883.

Roscoe, Thomas, *Wanderings and Excursions in North Wales*, London, C. Tilt & Co. Wrightson & Webb, Birmingham, Birmingham, 1836.

Rosenthal, Michael, Payne, Christina & Wilcox, Scott, eds., *Prospects for the Nation: Recent Essays in British Art 1750–1980*, Yale University Press, New Haven and London, 1997.

Rowan, Eric, *Some Miraculous Promised Land: J. D. Innes, Augustus John and Derwent Lees in North Wales 1910–1913*, exhibition catalogue, Mostyn Art Gallery, Llandudno, 1982.

Rowan, Eric, *Art in Wales: An Illustrated History 1850–1980*, Welsh Arts Council & University of Wales Press, Cardiff, 1985.

Ruskin, John, *Modern Painters Volume IV Of Mountain Beauty*, (1856) George Allen & Sons, London, 1910.

Sloan, Kim, *'A Noble Art' Amateur Artists and Drawing Masters c. 1600–1800'* exhibition catalogue, British Museum Press, London, 2000.

Solkin, David, *Richard Wilson and the British Landscape*, PhD thesis, Yale University, 1978.

Solkin, David, *Richard Wilson The Landscape of Reaction*, exhibition catalogue, Tate Gallery Publications, London, 1982.

Solly, Nathaniel Neal, *Memoir of the Life of David Cox with selections from his correspondence and some account of his works*, Chapman & Hall, London, 1873. (facsimile edition, Rodart Reproductions Ltd., London, 1973)

Staley, Alan, *The Pre-Raphaelite Landscape*, Clarendon Press, Oxford, 1973.

Taylor, Basil, *Joshua Cristall 1768–1847*, exhibition catalogue, HMSO & Victoria & Albert Museum, London, 1975.

Twitchell, James, *Romantic Horizons: Aspects of the Sublime in English Poetry and Painting 1770–1850*, University of Missouri Press, Columbia, 1983.

Vale, Edmund, *The Mail-Coach Men of the late eighteenth century*, (1960) David and Charles, Newton Abbot, 1967.

Walters, Gwynfryn, *The tourist and guide book literature of Wales 1770–1870, A descriptive and bibliographical survey with an analysis of the cartographic content and its content*, M.Sc. thesis, University of Wales, Aberystwyth, 1966.

Wilcox, Scott, *David Cox: His Development as a painter in Watercolours*, PhD thesis, Yale University, 1984.

Wilcox, Scott, *Sun, Wind and Rain: The Art of David Cox*, exhibition catalogue, Yale University Press, 2008.

Wildman, Stephen, *David Cox 1783–1859, A Bicentenary Exhibition*, exhibition catalogue, Birmingham Museum & Art Gallery, Birmingham, 1983.

Wilkinson, Gerald, *Turner's Early Sketchbooks*, Barrie & Jenkins, London, 1972.

Williams, Iolo, *Early English Watercolours and some Cognate Drawings by Artists Born not Later than 1785*, (1952) Redwood Press Ltd., Trowbridge & London, 1973.

Wilton, Andrew, & Lyles, Anne, *The Great Age of British Watercolours 1750–1880*, exhibition catalogue, Royal Academy of Arts, London & Prestal-Verlag Munich, Munich, 1993.

Wilton, Andrew, *The Life and Work of J. M. W. Turner*, Academy Editions, London, 1979.

Wilton, Andrew, *Turner in Wales*, exhibition catalogue, Llanudno, & Vivian Art Gallery & Museum, Swansea, 1984.

Wyndham, Henry Penruddocke, *A Tour through Monmouthshire and Wales. Made in the months of June and July 1774, and in the months of June, July and August 1777*, Salisbury, 1781 (illustrations by S. H. Grimm).

List of Illustrated Works with Credit Lines, Photographic Credits and Copyright Credits

Works are listed in plate order. Dimensions are given in centimetres, height before width. Owners of works have provided photographs unless otherwise indicated. Museum Credit lines are listed with the plate entry.

Introduction

Figure 1. Moses Griffith, The Journey to Snowdon, Frontispiece, 18.5 x 15, in Thomas Pennant, A Tour in Wales, London, 1784, private collection.

Chapter One
A View in Nant Peris: A Topographical Viewpoint

Plate number

1. Paul Sandby, Snowdon in Caernarvonshire, 1789, (first pub. 1779). engraving, 13 x 18.3, private collection.
2. Samuel Hieronymus Grimm, Dolbadarn Castle, engraving, 15.1 x 21, in Henry Penruddocke Wyndham, A Gentleman's Tour through Monmouthshire and Wales. Made in the months of June and July 1774, and in the months of June, July and August 1777, Salisbury, 1781, plate XIII. private collection.
3. Moses Griffith, A View in Nant Beris, engraving, 12.6 x 18.4, in Thomas Pennant, A Tour in Wales, The Journey to Snowdon, vol. 2, London, 1784, plate VIII. private collection.
4. Joseph Mallord William Turner, Lake Llanberis and Dolbadarn Castle with Snowdon Beyond, 1799, gouache, graphite and watercolour on paper 55.7 x 76.5, Tate Britain, (Credit Line) Turner Bequest, 1856.
5. Edmund Becker, View of Dolbadarn Castle with Snowdon Beyond, c.1808-12, wash drawing, 20 x 29, private collection.
6. Thomas Creswick, Dolbadarn Tower, engraving, 9.7 x 14.5, in Thomas Roscoe, Wanderings and Excursions in North Wales, London, 1836, plate XIX, private collection.

Chapter Two
Snowdon from Capel Curig: A Classical Viewpoint

7. Philippe Jacques de Loutherbourg, Snowdon from Capel Curig, a morning, 1787, oil on canvas, 134.5 x 200, (Credit Line) Yale Centre for British Art, Paul Mellon Collection.
8. Moses Griffith, The Summit of Snowdon from Capel Curig, engraving, 12.2 x 19, in Thomas Pennant, A Tour in Wales, The Journey to Snowdon, vol. 2, London, 1784, plate VII, private collection.
9. Joseph Mallord William Turner, View from Capel Curig towards Snowdon, the mountains under cloud, 1798, pencil and watercolour on paper, 22.5 x 33.2, Tate Britain, (Credit Line) From Hereford Court Sketchbook (Finberg XXXVIII), Turner Bequest 1856.
10. John Varley, Snowdon from Capel Curig, c.1805-1810, unfinished watercolour, 35.5 x 45.5, Victoria and Albert Museum, London. © Victoria and Albert Museum, London.
11. Edward Pugh, North-East View of Snowdon, 1813, aquatint print, 15 x 19.8, in Edward Pugh, Cambria Depicta: A Tour through North Wales Illustrated with Picturesque Views by a Native Artist, London, 1816, p. 114., private collection.
12. George Grainger Smith, Snowdon from Capel Curig, 1939, oil on board, 64.2 x 76.8, Walker Art Gallery, National Museums Liverpool. (Credit Line) Courtesy National Museums Liverpool, Walker Art Gallery.

Chapter Three
Views of Snowdon

13. Richard Wilson, Snowdon, c. 1764-5, graphite on paper, 20.6 x 32.1, Huntington Library, Art Collections and Botanical Gardens, Sir Bruce Ingram Collection. (Credit Line) Courtesy The Huntington Art Collections, San Marino, California.
14. Richard Wilson, Snowdon from Llyn Nantlle, 1765-6, oil on canvas, 101.6 x 127, Walker Art Gallery, National Museums Liverpool. Courtesy National Museums Liverpool, Walker Art Gallery.
15. John Warwick Smith, An Ascent of Snowdon, 1790, watercolour over graphite on paper, 13.8 x 20.8, British Museum. © The Trustees of the British Museum.
16. Joseph Mallord William Turner, Y Garn with Snowdon in the distance, from above Nantlle, 1799, gouache, graphite and watercolour on paper, 55.7 x 76.8, Tate Britain. Turner Bequest 1856.
17. Thomas Mann Baynes, Snowdon from Nantlle, c.1825,

lithograph, 10.2 x 15.3, in Rev. G.K.Freeman, Sketches in Wales; or a Diary of Three Walking Excursions in that Principality, in the years 1823, 1824, 1825, London, 1826, plate 13, private collection.

18. Joshua Cristall, Aber Llan from Plas Gwynant, c.1831, pen over traces of pencil on paper, 25.4 x 35.8, private collection.

19. Sidney Richard Percy, In Snowdonia, 1853, oil on canvas, 55.2 x 78.9, Tate Britain, purchased with assistance of the Abbot Fund 1996.

20. Henry Clarence Whaite, The Heart of Snowdon, c.1907, oil on canvas, 142.2 x 173.3, National Museums Liverpool. Courtesy National Museums Liverpool, Walker Art Gallery.

21. Kyffin Williams, Snowdon from Drws y Coed, c.1965, oil on canvas, 119.8 x 181.6, Bangor University Collection. Courtesy Bangor University Art Collection.

22. David Tress, Light Passing (Llyn Llydaw) Towards Snowdon, 2007, mixed media on paper, 57 x 77, Tabernacle Collection, Museum of Modern Art Wales. Machynlleth, Powys.

23. Robert A Newell, Clogwyn Du'r Arddu, 2012, oil on canvas, 106.7 x 152.5, collection of the artist.

Chapter Four
Sketching on the Move

24. Paul Sandby, View of the River Dee 3 Miles Short of Bala, with Cader - Idris Mountain near Dolgelli 30 Miles Distant, 1777, aquatint print, 23.7 x 31.4, drawn and published by Paul Sandby, London, private collection.

25. Cornelius Varley, Panorama of Cader Idris from Llanelltyd, NW, 1803, pencil and grey wash on paper, 26.7 x 43.5, Courtauld Institute of Art, London. The Samuel Courtauld Trust, The Courtauld Gallery, London.

26. ir John James Stewart, Cader Idris from the road between Barmouth and Dolgelly NW, c.1820, watercolour over traces of pencil, 10.5 x 15, private collection.

27. Thomas Tudor of Monmouth, Near Dolgelly, c. 1820, pencil and pen on paper, 13 x 22.5, private collection.

28. Joshua Cristall, the summit of Cader Idris, Dolgelly side, 1820, pencil on paper, 20 x 34, private collection.

29. Kevan Hopson, Cader Idris from near Llanelltyd, 2013, mixed media on paper, 25 x 27, private collection.

30. Matthew Wood, Snowdonia from Nebo, 2013, oil on board, 9 x 21, private collection.

Chapter Five
Views of Cader Idris

31. Richard Wilson, Llyn y Cau, Cader Idris, c. 1765-7, oil on canvas, 50 x 72, Tate Britain, presented by Sir Edward Marsh 1945.

32. Thomas Tudor, Cader Idris, 1802, pencil and wash on paper, 28.5 x 27.5, National Library of Wales, Aberystwyth. By permission of Llyfrgell Genedlaethol Cymru/National Library of Wales.

33. James Ward, Cader Idris on a Cloudy Day, 1807, pen and ink wash drawing, 8.6 x 16.5, private collection.

34. Samuel Jackson, Llyn y Cau, Cader Idris, c. 1833, watercolour on paper, 28 x 39, private collection.

35. David Cox, Mountain Heights, Cader Idris, c. 1850, watercolour over black chalk on paper, 47.8 x 74.6, National Gallery of Art, Washington DC, USA. The Armand Hammer Collection.

36. Herbert Edwin Pelham Hughes-Stanton, Cader Idris, 1918, oil on canvas, 41.2 x 54.9, Royal Albert Memorial Museum, Exeter, Courtesy Royal Albert Memorial Museum and Art Gallery, Exeter.

37. Tom Cross, Cader Idris from Tal-y-Llyn, 1994, watercolour and gouache on paper, 45.6 x 73.5, National Library of Wales, Aberystwyth. By permission of Llyfrgell Genedlaethol Cymru /National Library of Wales.

38. Pete Davis, Cader Idris, 1996, Selenium toned gelatin silver print, 38 x 56, private collection.

39. Peter Bishop, Cadair Idris and Llyn Cau, 1996, mixed media drawing on paper 58 x 82, National Library of Wales, Aberystwyth. By permission of Llyfrgell Genedlaethol Cymru /National Library of Wales.

Chapter Six
Pont Aberglaslyn: A Picturesque Viewpoint

40. Samuel Hieronymus Grimm, View of the Pass from Pont Aberglaslyn which divides Monmouth from Caernarvonshire, 1780, engraving, 21.5 x 15, in Henry Penruddocke Wyndham, A Gentleman's Tour Through Monmouthshire and Wales,

41. Moses Griffith, attributed, A Vignet of Pont Aber Glas Llyn, engraving, 9 x 11, in Thomas Pennant, A Tour in Wales, The Journey to Snowdon, vol. 2, London, 1784, plate XV., private collection.
42. Rev. William Henry Barnard, Pont Aberglaslyn, 1795, Graphite and watercolour on paper, 65.5 x 50, Tate Britain. Purchased as part of the Oppe Collection with assistance from the National Lottery through the Heritage Lottery Fund 1996.
43. Francis Nicholson, Pont Aberglaslyn, c. 1809, oil on canvas, 55.6 x 76, National Museum of Wales, Cardiff. © National Museum of Wales.
44. David Cox, Pont Aberglaslyn North Wales, 1836, engraving, 9.8 x 14, in Thomas Roscoe, Wanderings and Excursions in North Wales, London and Birmingham, 1836, plate XXVIII, f.p. 204, private collection.
45. Myles Birket Foster, Pont Aberglaslyn, c. 1858, engraving, 12.7 x 8, in Black's Picturesque Guide to North Wales, Edinburgh, 1886, f.p. 130, private collection.
46. Benjamin Williams Leader, The Pass of Aberglaslyn, 1871, oil on canvas, 56 x 48, Dudley Museum and Art Gallery. Courtesy Dudley Museum and Art Gallery, Dudley MBC.
47. Russell Gilder, A View from Pont Aberglaslyn, 2014, 144 x 104, charcoal on paper, private collection.

Chapter Seven
Llyn Idwal: A Sublime Viewpoint

48. George Fennel Robson, The Devil's Kitchen, Llyn Idwal, North Wales, c.1830, watercolour, 19.9 x 27.2, Whitworth Art Gallery, Manchester. The Whitworth, The University of Manchester.
49. David Cox, Llyn Idwal, 1836, engraving, 9.8 x 14, in Thomas Roscoe, Wanderings and Excursions in North Wales, London and Birmingham, 1836, plate XXIII, private collection.
50. Samuel Jackson, Llyn Idwal, Snowdonia, c. 1835, watercolour, 20.8 x 31.1, Fitzwilliam Museum, Cambridge. © Fitzwilliam Museum, Cambridge.
51. Edward Pugh, Nant Ffrancon, c. 1813, aquatint print, 14.8 x 20, in Edward Pugh, Cambria Depicta, London, 1816, f.p. 106. private collection.
52. Alfred William Hunt, Cwm Trifaen, The Track of an Ancient Glacier, 1857-8, oil on canvas, 60.3 x 90.8, Tate Britain. (Credit Line) Bequeathed by Miss Violet Hunt 1942.
53. Charles William Mansel Lewis, The Devil's Kitchen, Llyn Idwal,1882, oil on canvas, 97 x 184, Stradey Castle Collection, Llanelli, South Wales. By kind permission of Patrick Mansel Lewis.
54. John Piper, Cwm Idwal, 1949, ink, watercolour and charcoal on paper, 21.6 x 27.9, private collection. Private Collection / Bridgeman Images.
55. Kyffin Williams, Tryfan 2, c. 1981, oil on canvas, 50 x 110, Atkinson Art Gallery, Southport. Reproduced by kind permission of Sefton MBC Leisure Services Department, Arts and Cultural Services, Atkinson Art Gallery.
56. Peter Prendergast, Nant Ffrancon Valley, Summer, 1990, oil on canvas, 135 x 283, Bangor University Collection. Courtesy of Bangor University Art Collection.
57. David Woodford, Cwm Idwal from Ffynnon Lloer, 2008-2013, oil on board, 77 x 113, collection of the artist.

Chapter Eight
Arenig Fawr: A Painter's Mountain

58. James Dickson Innes, Arenig, 1911, ink and watercolour on paper, 25.4 x 35.6, Tate Britain. Presented by Mrs Innes 1921.
59. James Dickson Innes, Arenig, North Wales, 1913, oil on plywood panel, 86 x 114, Tate Britain. Presented by Rowland Burdon-Muller 1928.
60. Augustus Edwin John, Arenig Mountain, 1911-12, oil on canvas, 46 x 76, Glynn Vivian Art Gallery, Swansea. City and County of Swansea; Glynn Vivian Art Gallery Collection.
61. Augustus Edwin John, Llyn Treweryn, 1911-12, oil on wood, 31.6 x 40.7, Tate Britain. Courtesy Tate Britain.
62. Derwent Lees, Arenig Fawr, 1911, oil on wood panel, 24.5 x 35, The Potteries Museum and Art Gallery, Stoke on Trent. Image courtesy of The Potteries Museum and Art Gallery, Stoke on Trent.
63. Clyde Holmes, Billowing Cloud, Snowdonia, 1987, oil on board, 80 x 102, National Library of Wales, Aberystwyth. By permission of Llyfrgell Genedlaethol Cymru/National Library of Wales.

Chapter Nine
Betws-y-coed and its Mountain Scenery

64. David Cox, The river Llugwy above Betws-y-coed, North Wales, 1845, watercolour on paper, 21 x 28, private collection.

65. Frederick Henry Henshaw, Dinas Betws-y-coed, North Wales, 1851, oil on canvas, 71 x 91.5, Government Art Collection.
© Crown Copyright: UK Government Art Collection.

66. Alfred William Hunt, Dolwyddelan Castle North Wales, 1856, watercolour on paper, 27.4 x 38.4, British Museum, London.
© The Trustees of the British Museum.

67. Henry Clarence Whaite, The Rainbow, 1862, oil on canvas, 139.7 x 241.6, Nottingham City Museum. Nottingham City Museums and Galleries (Nottingham Castle)/Bridgeman Images.

68. Benjamin Williams Leader, Betws-y-Coed, c.1865, oil on mill board, 16.2 x 23.2, Victoria and Albert Museum, London.
© Victoria and Albert Museum, London.

69. Roland Vivian Pitchforth, Snowdonia, c. 1954, watercolour on paper, 47 x 62.5, private collection.

Photographic Plate Credits

Atkinson Art Gallery, Southport. 55.
Bangor University. 21, 56.
Richard Bishop Photography p.5, p.10, fig 1, 1, 2, 3, 6, 8, 11, 17, 18, 24, 26, 27, 29, 30, 33, 34, 40, 41, 44, 45, 47, 49, 51, 64, 69.
Bridgeman Images. 54, 67.
The British Museum 15, 66.
Courtauld Institute of Art / London. 25.
Pete Davis 38.
Dudley Museum and Art Gallery. 46.
Glynn Vivian Art Gallery, 60.
The Huntington Art Collections, San Marino, California. 13.
The Fitzwilliam Museum, Cambridge. 50,
Llyfrgell Genedlaethol Cymru / National Library of Wales. 32, 37, 39, 63.
National Gallery of Art, Washington 35.
National Museums Liverpool, Walker Art Gallery. 14.
National Museum of Wales. 43.
Robert A Newell 23.
Malcolm Payne, Colourfast Imaging. 5, 28.
The Potteries Museum and Art Gallery. 62.
Public Catalogue Foundation. 12. 20.
Royal Albert Memorial Museum, Exeter 36.
Dan Staveley Photography. 53.
Tate Images 4, 9, 16, 19, 31, 42, 52, 58, 59, 61.
David Tress. 22.
UK Government Art Collection. 65.
V&A Images. 10, 68.
Whitworth Art Gallery. 48.
Reuben Woodford. 57.
Yale Centre for British Art, Paul Mellon Collection 7.

Copyright Credits

Unless otherwise stated copyright resides with the artist or the estate of the artist. We have in each case made every effort to contact copyright holders and apologise if any omissions have occurred.

Tom Cross
    By kind permission of Pat Cross

F W Henshaw
    Crown Copyright: UK Government Art Collection

Clyde Holmes
    By kind permission of Malka Holmes

Augustus John
    Estate of Augustus John / The Bridgeman Art Library

Charles William Mansel Lewis
    By kind permission of Patrick Mansel Lewis

John Piper
    By kind permission of Clarissa Lewis

Peter Prendergast
    By kind permission of Lesley Prendergast